Simple Guide to Cryptography

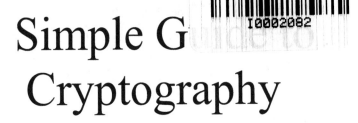

Practical Guide

A. De Quattro

Practical Guide to Cryptography

Introduction

In our increasingly digital and interconnected world, the importance of securing information cannot be overstated. With the everyday use of the internet for communication, banking, shopping, and numerous other activities, there exists a vital need for privacy, integrity, and authentication of data. This is where cryptography comes into play.

What is Cryptography?

Cryptography is the science of encoding and decoding information so that only authorized parties can access it. Derived from the Greek words "kryptos" (hidden) and "grapho" (to write), the term refers to various techniques and methodologies used to secure communication by converting plaintext — easily readable information — into ciphertext, which is obscured and incomprehensible without the appropriate decryption key. This practice not only protects the content of the information from unauthorized access but also ensures its authenticity and integrity.

Cryptography encompasses a wide range of techniques, from classical ciphers and codes to modern computational methods employing complex algorithms. The development of cryptography has gone hand in hand with technological advancements and the increasing necessity for secure communication. It's a vital aspect of cybersecurity and is used across various fields, including finance, healthcare, military, and personal communications.

Chapter 1: Definition and Importance

Definition of Cryptography

At its core, cryptography transforms readable data into a format that is secure from unauthorized access. This transformation can be achieved through several processes, including:

1. **Encryption**: The process of converting plaintext into ciphertext using algorithms and keys.

2. **Decryption**: The reverse process, where ciphertext is converted back into plaintext.

3. **Hashing**: Producing a fixed-size output (hash) from input data, ensuring data integrity and authenticity.

The complexity of modern cryptographic

systems arises from the algorithms employed and the length and randomness of the keys used in the encryption process. The stronger the algorithm and the longer and more unpredictable the key, the harder it is for attackers to decrypt the information without authorization.

Importance of Cryptography

The importance of cryptography can be highlighted through three primary goals, often referred to as the "CIA triad":

1. **Confidentiality**: Ensuring that information is only accessible to those authorized to view it. This prevents unauthorized parties from gaining access to sensitive data, which can be achieved through various encryption techniques.

2. **Integrity**: Protecting the information

from being altered in an unauthorized manner. Hash functions and digital signatures can be employed to verify that the information received is the same as the information sent.

3. **Authentication**: Ensuring that the parties involved in a communication are who they claim to be. Authentication methods, such as digital certificates and public-key infrastructures, help establish trust between users and systems.

The consequences of failing to implement robust cryptographic measures can be severe, including financial theft, data breaches, and loss of sensitive information. Notably, in the medical field, failures in data protection can lead to breaches of personal medical history, resulting in legal ramifications and loss of trust. As such, understanding the fundamentals of cryptography is essential for anyone involved in the digital realm.

History of Cryptography

The historical timeline of cryptography is rich and diverse, reflecting the development of human communication and the ongoing struggle between secrecy and surveillance.

1. **Ancient Civilizations**: The earliest forms of cryptography can be traced back to ancient Egypt, where hieroglyphics were sometimes used to encode messages. The Greeks and Romans, particularly with Julius Caesar's famous shift cipher (Caesar Cipher), played significant roles in the early development of cryptographic techniques.

2. **Medieval Period**: During the Middle Ages, cryptography became more sophisticated. The introduction of various ciphering techniques, including transposition ciphers and more complex substitution methods, marked significant advancements. The invention of the printing press made it

easier to disseminate ciphers, encouraging their use in both personal communication and state affairs.

3. **World Wars**: The World Wars significantly spurred advancements in cryptography, leading to the creation of complex machines for encoding and decoding messages. The Enigma machine, used by the Germans during World War II, is among the most famous examples. The efforts of cryptanalysts, particularly those at Bletchley Park, to break the Enigma code were crucial to the Allied victory.

4. **Post-war Era and the Digital Revolution**: The Cold War ushered in a new era for cryptography, as governments recognized its strategic importance. The development of public-key cryptography in the 1970s by Whitfield Diffie and Martin Hellman revolutionized the field, allowing secure communication without the need for exchanging private keys.

5. **The Modern Era**: With the rise of the internet and digital technology, cryptography has become indispensable. This period has seen the development of various encryption standards, such as the Advanced Encryption Standard (AES) and RSA encryption, which are widely used to secure online communications.

Applications in Modern Life

Cryptography is pervasive in modern life, underpinning a multitude of systems and practices that define how we communicate, transact, and interact online.

1. **Online Banking and E-Commerce**: Cryptographic protocols such as Secure Socket Layer (SSL) and Transport Layer Security (TLS) are fundamental to securing online transactions. When consumers input

sensitive information, such as credit card details, cryptography ensures that this data remains confidential as it travels across the internet.

2. **Email Security**: With the rise of email as a primary means of communication, cryptography has played a crucial role in protecting against eavesdropping and tampering. Encryption algorithms safeguard the contents of emails and authenticate the sender through digital signatures.

3. **Secure Messaging**: Messaging applications like Signal and WhatsApp utilize end-to-end encryption, ensuring that only the sender and recipient can read the messages. Even the service providers cannot access the content, thereby enhancing user privacy.

4. **Data Protection**: Businesses use cryptography to protect sensitive data stored on their servers and in the cloud. Techniques

such as full-disk encryption ensure that data remains secure, even if physical storage devices are lost or stolen.

5. **Digital Signatures and Certificates**: Digital signatures verify the authenticity and integrity of digital messages and documents, providing a tamper-proof way to confirm the identity of the sender. Digital certificates, issued by trusted authorities, provide users and systems with a way to authenticate each other.

6. **Blockchain Technology**: Cryptography is foundational to blockchain technology, securing the integrity of transactions and enabling decentralized systems. As cryptocurrencies have gained popularity, cryptographic principles have helped facilitate secure exchanges.

7. **Government and Military**: Cryptography is crucial in protecting national

security. Governments employ advanced cryptographic techniques to secure communication and safeguard sensitive information from potential threats.

8. **Healthcare**: In the healthcare sector, cryptographic methods protect patient records and medical history, ensuring confidentiality and compliance with regulations such as HIPAA (Health Insurance Portability and Accountability Act) in the United States.

9. **IoT Security**: As the Internet of Things (IoT) expands, securing devices and data becomes essential. Cryptographic techniques help protect the communications and data from smart devices, reducing vulnerabilities in an increasingly interconnected environment.

Conclusion

As we advance further into the information

age, the implications of cryptography will continue to evolve. It is crucial for individuals, organizations, and governments to stay informed about cryptographic technologies and best practices to safeguard their data and communication. The historical and modern significance of cryptography underscores its vital role in protecting our digital lives, making it an indispensable part of our security frameworks. In an ever-changing digital landscape, investing in cryptographic education and implementing robust safeguarding measures is essential to maintaining the confidentiality, integrity, and authenticity of our information.

Through an understanding of cryptography, we can better navigate the complexities of the digital world, counteract threats, and contribute to a safer, more secure society. Cryptography is not merely a tool; it is a shield protecting our most vital data and maintaining the trust that underpins all digital communications.

Chapter 2: Fundamentals of Cryptography

Cryptography is the cornerstone of secure communication in the modern world. It is an art as much as a science and serves as the guardian of sensitive information, ensuring that only authorized parties can access and interpret that information. In this chapter, we will explore the foundational principles of cryptography, focusing on symmetric and asymmetric encryption, hash functions, and the principles of randomness and key generation. Each of these components plays a vital role in securing data and maintaining confidentiality, integrity, and authentication.

2.1 Symmetric vs. Asymmetric Cryptography

The first fundamental distinction in cryptography is between symmetric and asymmetric encryption.

2.1.1 Symmetric Cryptography

Symmetric cryptography, also known as secret-key or private-key cryptography, involves the use of a single key that is shared between the parties involved in communication. Both the sender and receiver must possess the same key, which enables them to encrypt and decrypt messages. The key remains confidential and must be kept secret from any unauthorized entities.

Characteristics of Symmetric Cryptography:

1. **Key Management:** The main challenge in symmetric cryptography is the secure management and distribution of the keys. If the key is intercepted during transmission or if it is poorly managed, the security of the entire communication can be compromised.

2. **Performance:** Symmetric encryption

algorithms are generally faster than asymmetric algorithms, making them suitable for encrypting large volumes of data or for real-time communication where speed is critical.

3. **Algorithm Examples:** Common symmetric algorithms include the Data Encryption Standard (DES), Advanced Encryption Standard (AES), 3DES (Triple DES), Blowfish, and RC4. AES, in particular, has become the standard for many applications due to its balance of security and performance.

Applications of Symmetric Cryptography:

Symmetric cryptography is widely used in various applications requiring secure data transmission. It is often employed in:

- Securing communication channels: Protocols like TLS (Transport Layer Security) and SSL (Secure Sockets Layer) use symmetric cryptography to establish secure connections over the Internet.

- Disk encryption: Tools like BitLocker and FileVault use symmetric keys to encrypt sensitive data at rest.

- Secure file transfer: Protocols like SFTP (Secure File Transfer Protocol) utilize symmetric encryption for encrypting files during transmission.

2.1.2 Asymmetric Cryptography

Asymmetric cryptography, also known as public-key cryptography, employs two keys: a public key and a private key. The public key is shared openly and can be used by anyone to encrypt messages. However, only the holder of the corresponding private key can decrypt those messages. This dual-key approach provides a robust mechanism for both encryption and digital signatures.

Characteristics of Asymmetric Cryptography:

1. **Key Distribution:** One of the primary advantages of asymmetric cryptography is that it alleviates the challenges of key distribution. Since the public key can be shared freely, there is no need for a secure means of communicating the key between parties.

2. **Performance:** While offering enhanced security and flexibility, asymmetric encryption is computationally more intensive than symmetric encryption. As such, it is often used to encrypt small amounts of data or to exchange symmetric keys securely, which can then be used for faster symmetric encryption of larger datasets.

3. **Algorithm Examples:** Notable asymmetric algorithms include RSA (Rivest-

Shamir-Adleman), DSA (Digital Signature Algorithm), and ECC (Elliptic Curve Cryptography). RSA is particularly well-known and widely used for its robustness and straightforward implementation.

Applications of Asymmetric Cryptography:

Asymmetric cryptography is crucial in securing communications and establishing trust online. Key applications include:

- Secure email: Protocols such as PGP (Pretty Good Privacy) use asymmetric encryption to secure email communications.

- Digital signatures: Asymmetric cryptography is used to create digital signatures that verify the authenticity and integrity of messages or documents.

- SSL/TLS Certificates: Websites use asymmetric cryptography to secure connections and establish trust through certificate authorities.

2.1.3 Comparison and Hybrid Approaches

While symmetric and asymmetric cryptography serve different purposes, they are often used in conjunction—known as hybrid cryptography—where asymmetric techniques are used for secure key exchange, and symmetric techniques are employed for the actual data encryption. This approach ensures efficient performance while maintaining strong security.

Use Case Example:

Suppose Alice wants to send a confidential message to Bob. She can perform the following steps:

1. Bob generates a pair of asymmetric keys (public and private) and shares his public key with Alice.

2. Alice generates a symmetric key for a fast encryption algorithm (e.g., AES) and uses this key to encrypt her message.

3. Alice then encrypts the symmetric key using Bob's public key and sends both the encrypted message and the encrypted symmetric key to Bob.

4. Upon receiving the message, Bob uses his private key to decrypt the symmetric key and then uses this key to decrypt the message.

This hybrid approach leverages the strengths of both cryptographic methods.

2.2 Hash Functions and Their Importance

2.2.1 What Are Hash Functions?

A hash function is a mathematical algorithm that transforms input data (or a message) into a fixed-size string of characters, which is typically a representation of a number. This output is called a hash value (or digest). Hash functions are fundamental to various cryptographic protocols and provide several important features.

Characteristics of Hash Functions:

1. **Deterministic:** The same input will always produce the same hash output.

2. **Fixed Size:** Regardless of the size of the input, the output hash will always be of a predetermined length (e.g., SHA-256 produces a 256-bit hash).

3. **Efficiency:** Hash functions are designed to compute the hash value quickly.

4. **Pre-image Resistance:** It should be computationally infeasible to reverse the hash function to discover the original input from

the hash output.

5. **Collision Resistance:** It should be infeasible to find two different inputs that produce the same hash output.

6. **Avalanche Effect:** A small change in the input should produce a significantly different hash, indicating high sensitivity to input changes.

2.2.2 Importance of Hash Functions

Hash functions are critical in maintaining security and integrity across various applications:

1. **Data Integrity Checks:** Hash functions are used to verify that data has not been altered or corrupted, commonly employed in file verification and data integrity checks.

2. **Digital Signatures:** Hash functions are integral to the process of creating digital

signatures. The content of a document is hashed, and the hash output is then encrypted with the sender's private key to produce the signature. The recipient can verify the signature by decrypting it and comparing the hash with their own computation of the document's hash.

3. **Password Storage:** Hash functions are used to securely store passwords. Instead of saving plain-text passwords, systems store hashed passwords, making it difficult for an attacker to retrieve the original password even if the hash is compromised.

4. **Blockchain Technology:** Hash functions underpin blockchain technology, providing the means for secure and tamper-proof records. Each block in a blockchain contains a hash of the previous block, creating a secure chain of blocks.

2.2.3 Common Hash Functions

Several hash functions are widely used in

practice today:

- **MD5** (Message-Digest Algorithm 5): Once popular, but now considered broken due to vulnerabilities and susceptibility to collisions.

- **SHA (Secure Hash Algorithms):** Various iterations exist, including SHA-1 (now deprecated due to vulnerabilities) and SHA-2 (which includes SHA-224, SHA-256, SHA-384, and SHA-512). SHA-2 is widely used and regarded as secure.

- **SHA-3:** The latest member of the Secure Hash Standard, designed to complement SHA-2 and provide additional options for hash function implementations.

2.3 Randomness and Key Generation

2.3.1 The Role of Randomness in Cryptography

Randomness is a vital component in cryptography, especially in the generation of cryptographic keys, nonces, and other parameters that require a high degree of unpredictability to ensure security. True randomness is essential to prevent attacks that exploit predictable values.

Types of Randomness:

1. **True Randomness:** Generated from inherently random physical processes, such as electronic noise or radioactive decay. True random number generators (TRNGs) produce unpredictable outputs that are highly secure for cryptographic purposes.

2. **Pseudo-randomness:** Generated by algorithms called pseudo-random number generators (PRNGs), which produce sequences of numbers that appear random but are generated from a deterministic process. PRNGs require an initial seed value, and

while they can be efficient and sufficient for many applications, their predictability can become a vulnerability if the seed is known or guessed.

2.3.2 Key Generation Process

Generating cryptographic keys that are secure and unpredictable is crucial for protecting sensitive information. Proper key generation involves a few key considerations:

1. **Seed Value:** For PRNGs, a strong and unpredictable seed value must be provided. This seed can be derived from various sources of entropy, such as system time, mouse movements, or keyboard presses.

2. **Algorithm Selection:** Choosing an appropriate cryptographic algorithm and its associated security parameters is critical for key generation.

3. **Length of the Key:** Longer keys

provide a higher level of security, as they exponentially increase the number of possible key combinations, making brute-force attacks infeasible. Recommendations for key lengths may vary depending on the application and level of security required. For example, a minimum of 128 bits is often recommended for symmetric keys, while 2048 or 3072 bits may be considered for RSA keys.

4. **Storage and Management:** Once generated, keys must be securely stored and managed to prevent unauthorized access. Key management practices may involve the use of hardware security modules (HSMs), secure key storage formats, and policies for key lifecycle management.

2.3.3 Importance of Secure Key Generation

The security of cryptographic systems largely depends on the reliability of key generation processes. Weaknesses in randomness or key generation techniques can lead to potential vulnerabilities that attackers can exploit, leading to unauthorized access, data breaches, or compromised communications.

By ensuring that keys are generated in a secure and unpredictable manner, organizations can significantly enhance the protection of sensitive data. This aspect of cryptography is foundational and cannot be overlooked in the design of secure systems.

In this chapter, we have explored the fundamental principles of cryptography, focusing on the essential concepts of symmetric and asymmetric cryptography, the significance of hash functions, and the critical role of randomness in secure key generation. Understanding these principles lays the groundwork for appreciating how cryptography safeguards our digital lives, ensuring secure communication, data integrity, and overall trust in the information systems we use daily. As we continue to navigate an increasingly interconnected and digital landscape, the importance of these foundational principles will only grow.

Chapter 3: Number Theory

Fundamental Concepts

Number theory is a branch of pure mathematics devoted to the study of the integers and more broadly to the relationships between numbers. At its core, number theory explores the properties of numbers themselves, particularly focusing on prime numbers and factorization.

Prime Numbers

A **prime number** is defined as a natural number greater than 1 that cannot be formed by multiplying two smaller natural numbers. In other words, a prime number has exactly two distinct positive divisors: 1 and itself. For example, the numbers 2, 3, 5, 7, and 11 are all prime numbers, while the number 4 is not prime because it can be divided evenly by 2.

The distribution of prime numbers among natural numbers is a central topic in number theory. The **Fundamental Theorem of Arithmetic** states that every integer greater than 1 either is prime itself or can be uniquely factored into prime numbers, disregarding the order of the factors. For example, the integer 28 can be expressed as \(2^2 \times 7 \).

Primes play a crucial role in various mathematical applications, but their importance is magnified in the field of cryptography. This is largely due to the difficulty of factorizing large numbers, a challenge that forms the foundation of numerous encryption algorithms.

Factorization

Factorization is the process of breaking down a number into its constituent prime factors. For example, the number 30 can be factored into primes as \(2 \times 3 \times

5 \). The concept of factorization is critical in number theory and has implications beyond pure mathematics, particularly in computer science and cryptography.

Efficient algorithms for factorization are essential for breaking certain encryption schemes. The time it takes to factor a number into its prime components grows significantly as the number increases. For example, while 15 can be factored relatively quickly (as 3×5), factorizing a number like $(\ semiprime = 1,000,000,000,019 \)$ (a product of two large primes) can be computationally intensive, even with modern technology.

This computational difficulty underpins several cryptographic protocols, particularly in public-key cryptography, where a user can share a public key (based on the product of two large primes) while keeping their private key (the two prime factors) secret.

Euler's Theorem and the Chinese Remainder Theorem

Two fundamental results in number theory that find significant applications in cryptography are **Euler's theorem** and the **Chinese Remainder Theorem (CRT)**.

Euler's Theorem

Euler's theorem states that if \(a \) and \(n \) are coprime (i.e., their greatest common divisor (gcd) is 1), then:

\[
a^{\phi(n)} \equiv 1 \, (\text{mod} \, n)
\]

where \(\phi(n) \) is Euler's totient function, which counts the number of integers up to \

(n \) that are coprime to \(n \).

Example: Let's say \(n = 10 \). The numbers less than 10 that are coprime to 10 are 1, 3, 7, and 9. Therefore, \(\phi(10) = 4 \). If we let \(a = 3 \) (which is coprime to 10), we have:

\[
3^{4} \equiv 1 \, (\text{mod} \, 10)
\]

To see this:

- \(3^1 = 3 \)

- \(3^2 = 9 \)

- \(3^3 = 27 \equiv 7 \, (\text{mod} \, 10) \)

- \(3^4 = 81 \equiv 1 \, (\text{mod} \, 10) \)

Euler's theorem is foundational for creating public key cryptographic systems such as RSA, where the encryption and decryption processes rely heavily on properties derived from modular arithmetic and the relationships established by Euler's theorem.

Chinese Remainder Theorem

The Chinese Remainder Theorem provides a way to solve systems of simultaneous congruences with distinct moduli. Specifically, if one has several equations of the form:

\[

x \equiv a_1 \, (\text{mod} \, n_1)

\]

\[

x \equiv a_2 \, (\text{mod} \, n_2)

\]

\[

\vdots

\]

\[

x \equiv a_k \, (\text{mod} \, n_k)

\]

where \(n_1, n_2, \ldots, n_k \) are pairwise coprime, then there exists a unique solution modulo \(N = n_1 n_2 \ldots n_k \).

The CRT is powerful in cryptography, particularly in the implementation of RSA. When large integers are used, the CRT allows for more efficient computation during encryption and decryption processes. By working modulo smaller primes, one can streamline calculations that would be complex if done directly with the larger numbers involved.

Applications in Cryptography

The relevance of number theory—especially the concepts of prime numbers, factorization, Euler's theorem, and the Chinese Remainder Theorem—cannot be overstated in the realm of cryptography. The security of several widely-used cryptographic systems is rooted deeply in these mathematical principles.

RSA Encryption

One of the most famous encryption algorithms in public key cryptography is RSA (Rivest–Shamir–Adleman). RSA utilizes the properties of prime numbers and modular arithmetic to achieve secure communication. The steps in RSA are as follows:

1. **Key Generation**:

- Select two distinct large prime numbers, p and q.

- Compute $n = pq$, which will be used as the modulus for both the public and private keys.

- Calculate $\phi(n) = (p-1)(q-1)$.

- Choose an integer e, such that $1 < e < \phi(n)$ and $\text{gcd}(e, \phi(n)) = 1$. This e becomes part of the public key.

- Determine d as the modular multiplicative inverse of e modulo $\phi(n)$. The value d serves as the private key.

2. **Encryption**:

- A sender who wants to communicate a message m will compute the ciphertext c using the public key (e, n):

$$
c \equiv m^e \, (\text{mod} \, n)
$$

3. **Decryption**:

  - The receiver, who knows the private key d, can retrieve m from c using:

$$
m \equiv c^d \, (\text{mod} \, n)
$$

The security of RSA hinges upon the difficulty of factoring the large product n. While e and n are public, the primes p and q are kept secret. If an adversary could efficiently factor n back into p and q, they could compute $\phi(n)$ and subsequently determine d, thus compromising the entire scheme.

Digital Signatures

Number theory is also employed in digital signature schemes, which enable a sender to guarantee the authenticity of a message. Using algorithms like RSA or DSA (Digital Signature Algorithm), the sender can create a signature for a message by encrypting a hash of the message with their private key. The recipient, upon receiving the signed message, can verify the signature using the corresponding public key, which provides assurance that the message has not been altered and genuinely originates from the sender.

Number theory serves as the backbone of modern cryptographic systems. The properties of prime numbers, the complexities of factorization, and the applications of Euler's theorem and the Chinese Remainder Theorem not only enrich mathematical understanding but also empower secure communications in our increasingly digital world. As algorithmic advancements and computing capabilities continue to evolve, the interplay between number theory and cryptography will remain a dynamic and critical area of study, responding to new challenges and opportunities in security and privacy. The future holds many possibilities, with number theory challenging cryptographers to constantly innovate to keep pace with emerging threats to secure information.

Chapter 4: Symmetric Cryptography

Symmetric Cryptography Overview

Symmetric cryptography, also known as secret-key cryptography, employs a single key for both encryption and decryption processes. This key must remain confidential between the parties involved for secure communication. The primary advantage of symmetric cryptography is its efficiency, particularly with large amounts of data, making it suitable for environments where speed is crucial.

However, the cornerstone challenge lies in the secure distribution of the symmetric key itself. If the key is intercepted during transmission or made accessible to unauthorized parties, the security afforded by the encryption is compromised. Consequently, robust methods for key exchange, such as the Diffie-Hellman key exchange or public-key infrastructure

(PKI), are crucial components of a secure symmetric encryption system.

Symmetric Encryption Algorithms

Within the realm of symmetric cryptography, various algorithms have been developed to encrypt and decrypt data. This chapter discusses two of the most prominent symmetric encryption algorithms: DES (Data Encryption Standard) and AES (Advanced Encryption Standard), as well as the distinctions between block and stream ciphers.

DES (Data Encryption Standard)

Overview

Introduced in the 1970s, DES was one of the first encryption standards widely adopted for securing electronic data. Developed by IBM and later endorsed by the National Institute of Standards and Technology (NIST), DES utilizes a symmetric key and operates on 64-bit blocks of data, employing a key length of 56 bits. While DES was once considered secure, advances in computing power have rendered it insecure against brute-force attacks.

Technical Structure

DES operates through a series of complex transformations involving substitution and permutation. The encryption process consists of 16 rounds of processing, wherein the data block undergoes expansion, substitution using S-boxes (which provide non-linearity), and permutation. Each round utilizes a subkey derived from the original key, which is generated through a key scheduling algorithm.

1. **Key Generation**: The original 56-bit key is initially permuted and split into two

halves. In each of the subsequent rounds, the halves are rotated and combined with the S-boxes to create round subkeys.

2. **Initial Permutation**: The 64-bit plaintext undergoes an initial permutation before entering the subsequent rounds.

3. **Feistel Function**: The main operation involves the Feistel function, which applies the round subkey to one half of the data and combines it with the other half using an XOR operation.

4. **Final Permutation**: After 16 rounds, the data undergoes a final permutation, producing the 64-bit ciphertext.

Security Concerns

The increasing availability of powerful

computing resources has led to the realization that a 56-bit key is vulnerable to exhaustive search techniques. In 1998, a team successfully cracked DES in a mere 56 hours, prompting NIST to retire DES and replace it with a more secure standard.

AES (Advanced Encryption Standard)

Overview

Accepted in 2001, AES was established as a replacement for DES to provide a higher level of security and efficiency. It is based on the Rijndael algorithm, developed by Belgian cryptographers Vincent Rijmen and Joan Daemen. AES supports key lengths of 128, 192, and 256 bits and operates on 128-bit blocks of data, making it significantly more resilient against attacks compared to its predecessor.

Technical Structure

The AES algorithm employs a series of transformations during its encryption and decryption processes, which can be described in four primary steps:

1. **Key Expansion**: The original key is expanded into an array of key schedules for each round of encryption.

2. **Initial Round**: AES begins with an initial round involving the AddRoundKey operation, where the plaintext is XORed with the first round key.

3. **Main Rounds**: The main operation consists of several rounds (10 for 128-bit keys, 12 for 192-bit keys, and 14 for 256-bit keys). Each round includes:

    - **SubBytes**: Each byte of the state array

is substituted using an S-box.

   - **ShiftRows**: The rows of the state are shifted cyclically to the left.

   - **MixColumns**: The columns of the state array are mixed through a linear transformation.

   - **AddRoundKey**: The state is XORed with the current round key.

4. **Final Round**: The last round omits the MixColumns step, finishing with the AddRoundKey operation.

Security Features

The security of AES is significant, with a larger key space providing resilience against brute-force attacks. For instance, AES-128 provides 2^{128} potential key combinations, while AES-256 provides an estimated 2^{256} combinations. Additionally, AES has been resistant to known cryptographic attacks, including differential and linear cryptanalysis, making it an industry standard for encryption applications ranging from securing wireless communication to file encryption.

Block Ciphers vs. Stream Ciphers

Asymmetric cryptography can further be categorized into two types: block ciphers and stream ciphers. Each approach has its own strengths and weaknesses, influencing their applications in various security protocols.

Block Ciphers

Block ciphers encrypt data in fixed-size blocks – typically 64 or 128 bits. The input data is padded if it isn't an exact multiple of the block size. Block ciphers operate in various modes of operation to handle blocks of data securely:

1. **Electronic Codebook (ECB)**: The simplest mode where each block is encrypted independently, but it reveals patterns and is not recommended for most applications.

2. **Cipher Block Chaining (CBC)**: Each block is XORed with the preceding block's ciphertext before encryption, providing better security through dependency on previous blocks.

3. **Counter (CTR)**: Instead of chaining, each block is encrypted with a counter value that incrementally changes, making it more suitable for parallel processing and streaming data.

4. **Output Feedback (OFB)** and **Cipher Feedback (CFB)**: These modes convert a block cipher into a stream cipher, enabling encryption of smaller units of data.

Block ciphers are typically preferred in

applications where the integrity of data blocks is critical, such as database encryption and securing file systems.

Stream Ciphers

Stream ciphers encrypt data as a continuous stream of bits, usually by XORing the plaintext with a key stream generated from the key. Because of their reliance on algorithms that produce a pseudo-random sequence, stream ciphers often achieve faster processing speeds than block ciphers.

Some popular stream ciphers include RC4 and Salsa20. However, stream ciphers can be more sensitive to key management issues since the same key must not be reused. If it is, security can be compromised, allowing an attacker to reveal plaintext patterns.

Symmetric cryptography plays a pivotal role in ensuring secure communication in today's digital landscape. DES, once a cornerstone of information security, became outdated due to advancements in computing power, leading to the adoption of AES, which provides higher levels of security with more robust key management practices.

Understanding the nuances of symmetric cryptography, including the various algorithms, operational modes, and the strengths and weaknesses of block and stream ciphers, is crucial for any professional engaged in cybersecurity, cryptography, or information protection. As technology continues to evolve, so too will the methods employed to secure sensitive information, underscoring the necessity for constant education and adaptation in this dynamic field.

In practice, a combination of symmetric and asymmetric cryptographic techniques is often employed to create a comprehensive security framework, leveraging the strengths of each to mitigate vulnerabilities and enhance data security in an interconnected world. With the continuous advancement of cryptographic research and the ongoing evolution of cyber threats, keeping abreast of developments in symmetric cryptography remains essential for ensuring the confidentiality, integrity, and authenticity of data.

Symmetric cryptography remains a vital and foundational element of data security, providing fundamental tools for protecting sensitive information against a host of threats in an increasingly complex digital environment.

Chapter 5: Modes of Operation

Cryptography is an essential component of modern information security, ensuring that sensitive data remains confidential and integral. In this chapter, we will delve into different modes of operation for block ciphers, specifically focusing on Electronic Codebook (ECB), Cipher Block Chaining (CBC), and Counter Mode (CTR). Each of these modes has its own unique characteristics, advantages, and disadvantages, which will be discussed in depth to provide a comprehensive understanding of how they function and when to utilize them effectively.

5.1 Electronic Codebook (ECB)

Electronic Codebook (ECB) mode is one of the simplest and most straightforward methods of encrypting data using block ciphers. In ECB, the plaintext is divided into blocks of fixed size (commonly 128 bits or 16 bytes), and each block is encrypted independently using the same encryption key. The resulting ciphertext blocks can then be sent, stored, or transmitted without any additional processing.

5.1.1 How ECB Works

1. **Plaintext Division**: The plaintext message is divided into blocks of equal length. If the plaintext length is not a multiple of the block size, padding may be applied (e.g., using PKCS#7 padding) to ensure that the last block matches the required size.

2. **Encryption**: Each block of plaintext is encrypted individually using the block cipher algorithm and the secret key. For example, if we use AES as our block cipher with a key size of 128 bits, each 128-bit block of plaintext is transformed into a 128-bit block of ciphertext.

3. **Output**: The ciphertext is generated by concatenating all the encrypted blocks. There is no interdependence between the blocks, meaning that if two blocks of plaintext are identical, the corresponding ciphertext blocks will also be identical.

5.1.2 Advantages of ECB

- **Simplicity**: The mechanics of ECB are straightforward and easy to implement. Each block is treated separately, making it simple to parallelize the encryption process.

- **Efficiency**: Due to the independent nature of block encryption, ECB can be efficient in environments where the encryption speed is a priority, particularly in hardware implementations.

- **Ease of Application**: ECB is relatively easy to apply for situations where the same data may need to be encrypted multiple times with the same key without the overhead of maintaining state or initialization vectors.

5.1.3 Disadvantages of ECB

Despite its advantages, ECB has significant security flaws:

- **Pattern Leaks**: The most critical issue with ECB is that the independent encryption of blocks allows for patterns in the plaintext to be visible in the ciphertext. If the same block of plaintext is encrypted multiple times, the same block of ciphertext will result, leading to potential leakage of information.

- **Lack of Confidentiality**: Since ECB does not use any form of chaining or feedback, attackers can exploit the predictable nature of the output. An attacker who observes the ciphertext can deduce information about the plaintext if certain blocks are known or can be guessed.

- **Less Robustness Against Modifications**: Since blocks are independent, if an attacker modifies a block of ciphertext, only that corresponding block of plaintext will be affected upon decryption. This allows for potential manipulation of data without detection.

In summary, while ECB is an easy-to-use and efficient mode of operation for block ciphers, its significant vulnerabilities make it unsuitable for most practical applications where data confidentiality is paramount.

5.2 Cipher Block Chaining (CBC)

In response to the weaknesses found in ECB, Cipher Block Chaining (CBC) mode was developed. CBC enhances the security of block ciphers by introducing a mechanism that binds the encryption of each plaintext block to the previous ciphertext block.

5.2.1 How CBC Works

1. **Initialization Vector (IV)**: CBC requires the use of a random or pseudo-random initialization vector (IV) that is the same size as the block (e.g., 128 bits for AES). The IV is not secret but must be unique for each encryption session to ensure that identical plaintexts produce different ciphertexts.

2. **Plaintext Division**: Like ECB, plaintext is divided into blocks of the same size. If the last block is not of the proper size, padding is applied.

3. **Chaining Process**: The first plaintext block is XORed with the IV before

encryption. The result is then encrypted to produce the first ciphertext block. For every subsequent block, the corresponding ciphertext block from the previous step is XORed with the current plaintext block before encryption:

- For the first block:

  `C1 = E_k(P1 ⊕IV)`

- For the second block:

  `C2 = E_k(P2 ⊕C1`)

  - This process continues for all blocks of plaintext.

4. **Output**: The concatenated ciphertext blocks are the final output. Each ciphertext block is dependent on its corresponding plaintext block and all preceding blocks, providing added security.

5.2.2 Advantages of CBC

- **Enhanced Security**: By chaining the blocks together, CBC ensures that the encryption of each block is dependent on the previous block, which mitigates the risk of pattern leaks and makes encryption more secure.

- **Randomization**: Even if the same plaintext is encrypted multiple times, the introduction of the random IV guarantees that the resulting ciphertext will differ each time, providing better confidentiality.

- **Resistance to Block Manipulation**: Because the decryption of each block relies on the previous ciphertext block, an error in one block causes subsequent blocks to be incorrectly decrypted, helping to detect unauthorized modifications.

5.2.3 Disadvantages of CBC

Despite its advantages, CBC has some drawbacks:

- **Padding Overhead**: CBC often requires padding, which can lead to inefficiencies and the possible need for additional processing if the plaintext is not a multiple of the block size.

- **Sequential Processing**: The chaining mechanism necessitates that the blocks be processed sequentially, which involves serialization of the encryption process. This can become a performance issue in high-speed applications where parallel processing is preferred.

- **IV Management**: The unique IV must

be securely managed and communicated along with the ciphertext. Improper handling of the IV can lead to vulnerabilities, and its reuse across sessions can compromise security.

Overall, CBC is a widely used operation mode that addresses many of the weaknesses found in ECB, making it suitable for a variety of applications where data confidentiality is critical.

5.3 Counter Mode (CTR)

Counter mode (CTR) operates differently from both ECB and CBC and is particularly effective in high-speed applications because it allows for parallel processing of ciphertext blocks. Rather than chaining ciphertext blocks together, CTR mode uses a counter that generates a unique keystream for each block of plaintext.

5.3.1 How CTR Works

1. **Initialization**: Similar to CBC, CTR mode begins with an initialization vector (IV) along with a counter that is set to a starting value (typically the IV).

2. **Keystream Generation**: Instead of encrypting the plaintext blocks directly, CTR mode encrypts a nonce (the IV concatenated with the counter) using the block cipher with the secret key to produce a keystream:

   - `Keystream = E_k(IV || Counter)`

   This step is repeated, incrementing the counter for each block of plaintext.

3. **XOR Operation**: The keystream generated from the corresponding counter value is then XORed with each plaintext block

to produce the ciphertext:

- For the first block:

`C1 = P1 ⊕Keystream(IV || CTR)`

- For the second block:

`C2 = P2 ⊕Keystream(IV || CTR + 1)`

- This process continues for all blocks.

4. **Output**: Like the previous modes, the output is a concatenation of all ciphertext blocks.

5.3.2 Advantages of CTR

- **Parallel Processing**: Since each block of ciphertext is independent of the others, CTR allows for parallel encryption and decryption, which significantly enhances performance, especially in multi-core or distributed computing environments.

- **No Padding Requirement**: Unlike CBC, CTR mode does not require padding since it operates on variable-length data. This eliminates the overhead associated with padding issues and allows for more flexible handling of plaintext sizes.

- **Randomization of Ciphertext**: As with CBC, using a unique IV for each encryption session ensures that the same plaintext encrypted multiple times will produce different ciphertext outputs.

5.3.3 Disadvantages of CTR

Despite its advantages, CTR mode has some potential drawbacks:

- **Counter Management**: The counter must be unique and never reused with the same IV. Reusing the IV-counter combination can lead to severe vulnerabilities, including the potential for recovering plaintext data through keystream reuse.

- **Security Implications**: If an attacker knows enough plaintext-ciphertext pairs, they might be able to discover information about the keystream, leading to security threats.

- **Potential for Error Propagation**: Similar to ECB, if any ciphertext block is altered, the corresponding plaintext block may become unreadable upon decryption, but the effect does not cascade (unlike in CBC).

In summary, Counter mode is a highly efficient and flexible mode of operation that leverages the strengths of parallel processing without the need for padding. It is particularly useful in scenarios that demand high throughput and low latency, such as streaming media or fast network communications.

In this chapter, we have explored three principal modes of operation for block ciphers: ECB, CBC, and CTR. Each mode presents unique attributes, merits, and drawbacks that make them suitable for different applications.

- **ECB** is simple and fast but fundamentally flawed in its security due to the lack of diffusion in ciphertext, making it unsuitable in modern cryptographic applications.

- **CBC** offers better security through the incorporation of feedback from previous ciphertext blocks but is limited by its sequential processing requirement and padding overhead.

- **CTR** mode balances efficiency and security, allowing for parallel encryption while maintaining robust confidentiality, which is particularly well-suited for high-speed applications.

Understanding these operational modes is critical for selecting the appropriate encryption strategy for a given application, ensuring that it meets the necessary security requirements while performing optimally under various constraints. As cryptography continues to evolve, new modes and enhancements will likely emerge to address the limitations of existing techniques while delivering improved performance and security.

Chapter 6: Key Management in Cryptography

Key management is a crucial component of cryptographic systems, as it encompasses the generation, distribution, storage, usage, and destruction of encryption keys. Effective key management ensures the confidentiality, integrity, and authenticity of information secured by cryptographic methods. In this chapter, we will cover two essential aspects of key management: key generation and distribution, and access control.

Key Generation and Distribution

1. Key Generation

Key generation refers to the process by which cryptographic keys are produced. The security of the cryptographic system is directly linked to the randomness and unpredictability of the generated keys. In general, there are two main types of key generation methods: deterministic and probabilistic.

- **Deterministic Key Generation**: In this method, keys are derived from a fixed set of parameters or inputs. Deterministic algorithms can lead to predictability in key generation, which poses a substantial security risk. Therefore, it is primarily used in systems where the predictability of the key does not compromise security (for instance, in some symmetric algorithms).

- **Probabilistic Key Generation**: This method leverages randomness to create keys that are difficult to predict or replicate. Randomness is typically sourced from various entropy sources, including physical processes (hardware noise), system events (mouse movements), and user inputs. Probabilistic key generation is critical for both symmetric and asymmetric algorithms, particularly in ensuring that the keys are unique and not susceptible to attacks.

To facilitate robust key generation, certain standards and best practices should be adhered to:

- **Use of Approved Random Number Generators (RNGs)**: RNGs must meet specific criteria—such as those defined by NIST (National Institute of Standards and Technology)—to ensure their randomness and unpredictability. A common choice is Cryptographically Secure Pseudo-Random Number Generators (CSPRNGs), which are designed to withstand cryptographic attacks.

- **Regular Key Updates**: Regularly updating keys is essential to mitigate risks due to potential compromises. The frequency of key updates depends on several factors, including the sensitivity of the data, the threat landscape, and compliance requirements.

- **Key Length Considerations**: Longer keys provide better security against brute-force attacks; therefore, selecting an appropriate key length based on the algorithm used and expected computational capabilities is vital. As computational power increases, the standards for acceptable key lengths evolve (e.g., AES-256 is commonly recommended for robust security).

2. Key Distribution

Once keys are generated, the next step is their secure distribution to authorized parties. Key distribution can be performed using various methods, each with its advantages and disadvantages:

- **Symmetric Key Distribution**: In symmetric cryptography, the same key is used for both encryption and decryption. Thus, securely sharing the key with legitimate parties is critical. The most commonly used methods for symmetric key distribution include:

- **Key Exchange Protocols**: Protocols like Diffie-Hellman enable parties to create a shared secret over an insecure channel. The exchange of the public keys allows parties to derive the same shared secret without transmitting it directly.

- **Secure Channels**: Secure channels like TLS/SSL can be used to transmit symmetric keys along with the data. This method ensures that the key is encrypted during transmission, protecting it from eavesdropping.

- **Asymmetric Key Distribution**: In asymmetric cryptography, different keys are used for encryption and decryption. Public-key infrastructure (PKI) facilitates the distribution of public keys while keeping private keys secure. Key distribution methods in asymmetric cryptography include:

- **Digital Certificates**: Certifying authority (CA) issues digital certificates that validate the ownership of public keys. A digital certificate contains the public key along with the identity of the owner, verified using the CA's private key.

- **Web of Trust**: This decentralized model relies on individuals to vouch for one another's keys. Users can sign others' public keys to establish trust without the need for a central authority, allowing for greater flexibility.

3. The Role of Key Management Systems (KMS)

Key Management Systems play a pivotal role in streamlining and securing key generation, distribution, storage, and management processes. A KMS provides a unified environment for handling cryptographic keys while ensuring compliance with various security standards (like GDPR, HIPAA, etc.).

Key functions of a KMS include:

- **Centralized Key Repository**: A KMS offers a centralized location to store keys securely, often with role-based access controls to ensure only authorized users can access sensitive keys.

- **Audit Logging**: KMS solutions maintain detailed logs of all key usage, including generation, access, and expiration, enabling organizations to monitor and review key activity for compliance and security audits.

- **Automated Key Rotation**: The KMS can automate the process of key rotation based on predefined policies, reducing human errors and mitigating risks associated with key staleness.

- **Integration with Existing Systems**: A KMS should be able to integrate with existing applications and infrastructure, allowing seamless key operations across multiple systems and enhancing overall security.

Access Control

Access control refers to the policies and mechanisms that prevent unauthorized users from accessing or manipulating cryptographic keys and the data they protect. Robust access control is critical for ensuring that only authorized personnel can handle cryptographic functions, thereby safeguarding sensitive information.

1. Types of Access Control Models

Various access control models can be applied to manage access to cryptographic keys:

- **Discretionary Access Control (DAC)**: In this model, the owner of the key determines who has access and what type of access permissions are granted. While DAC provides flexibility, it also poses the risk of key exposure due to potential negligent practices.

- **Mandatory Access Control (MAC)**: MAC enforces policies that restrict user access based on predefined security classifications. No user can alter access controls, thereby minimizing the risk of key compromise.

- **Role-Based Access Control (RBAC)**: In RBAC, access rights are granted based on user roles within the organization. Roles define what users can do with the keys, streamlining permissions according to job responsibilities. This helps in minimizing the exposure of sensitive keys and aligning access patterns with organizational hierarchies.

2. Best Practices for Key Access Control

Implementing best practices for access control enhances the security of cryptographic keys and the systems that utilize them:

- **Least Privilege Principle**: Access permissions should be granted based on the principle of least privilege, allowing users the minimum level of access necessary to perform their duties. This minimizes the attack surface and limits the potential for insider threats.

- **Multi-Factor Authentication (MFA)**: Employing MFA adds an additional layer of security by requiring users to verify their identity through multiple means (e.g., a password and a hardware token) before accessing cryptographic keys.

- **Regular Audits and Reviews**: Organizations should conduct regular audits of access permissions to ensure compliance with security policies. Regular reviews help identify and revoke unnecessary permissions, which can reduce the risk of unauthorized access.

- **Incident Response Plan**: In the event of a key compromise, an organization should have a robust incident response plan in place. This includes procedures for alerting affected parties, revoking compromised keys, and recovering in a timely manner.

3. Training and Awareness

Educating personnel on the importance of key

management and access control is vital.
Regular training sessions ensure that
employees understand the risks associated
with cryptographic keys and how to handle
them securely. Awareness programs can
reinforce best practices and invite a culture of
security within the organization.

Key management and access control are
integral to the security of cryptographic
systems. The processes involved in key
generation and distribution must be executed
meticulously to prevent attacks and data
breaches. By leveraging key management
systems and implementing robust access
control measures, organizations can secure
their cryptographic keys and thereby protect
sensitive information from unauthorized
access and misuse.

As technology continues to evolve, the

strategies for key management and access control must also adapt, maintaining a stringent approach to safeguarding cryptographic assets. By employing best practices and continuously improving security measures, we can achieve a resilient cryptographic infrastructure that effectively counteracts threats in our increasingly digital world.

Chapter 7: Asymmetric Cryptography

Asymmetric cryptography, also known as public-key cryptography, represents a significant advancement over symmetric cryptography, which relies on a single secret key for both encryption and decryption. In contrast, asymmetric cryptography uses a pair of keys: a public key, which can be shared with anyone, and a private key, which must be kept secret. This method addresses some of the key challenges in secure communication, including key distribution and management.

Overview of Asymmetric Cryptography

The primary advantage of asymmetric cryptography is that it allows users to communicate securely without the need to share a secret key in advance. Instead, each user has a public key, which is available to anyone, and a private key, which only the user knows. When one party wants to send a secure message to another, they encrypt the message using the recipient's public key. Only the recipient can decrypt it using their corresponding private key. This approach also facilitates digital signatures, allowing users to verify authenticity and integrity.

In this chapter, we will explore the fundamental algorithms of asymmetric cryptography, focusing on RSA (Rivest-Shamir-Adleman), DSA (Digital Signature Algorithm), and Diffie-Hellman for key exchange. Additionally, we will touch upon hashing, an essential component in modern cryptographic practices, even though it does not strictly fall under the category of asymmetric cryptography.

RSA (Rivest-Shamir-Adleman)

Overview of RSA

RSA is perhaps the most widely known and used asymmetric cryptographic algorithm. It was invented in 1977 by Ron Rivest, Adi Shamir, and Leonard Adleman. The algorithm is based on the mathematical properties of prime numbers and modular arithmetic.

Key Generation

The first step in using RSA is generating a pair of keys: the public key and the private key. The process involves the following steps:

1. **Select Two Prime Numbers**: Choose two distinct prime numbers, p and q. The security of RSA relies heavily on the difficulty of factoring the product of these large primes.

2. **Calculate n**: Compute n as the product of p and q (i.e., $n = p \times q$). The value n is used as part of the

public key.

3. **Compute Euler's Totient Function**: Calculate $\phi(n)$, which represents the number of integers up to n that are coprime with n. It can be computed as $\phi(n) = (p-1)(q-1)$.

4. **Choose the Public Exponent**: Select an integer e such that $1 < e < \phi(n)$ and e is coprime to $\phi(n)$. A common choice for e is 65537 due to its properties that facilitate efficient encryption.

5. **Calculate the Private Exponent**: Determine d as the modular multiplicative inverse of e modulo $\phi(n)$, satisfying the equation $d \cdot e \equiv 1 \mod \phi(n)$.

The public key is then represented as the pair (n, e), while the private key is represented as (n, d).

Encryption and Decryption

With RSA keys generated, we can proceed to encrypt and decrypt messages.

- **Encryption**: To encrypt a plaintext message M, first represent M as an integer in the range 0 to $n-1$. The ciphertext C is computed using the public key:

$$
C = M^e \mod n
$$

- **Decryption**: Upon receiving the ciphertext C, the recipient uses their private key to retrieve the original message:

$$
M = C^d \mod n
$$

Because the mathematical foundation of RSA is based on the difficulty of factoring large integers, increasing the key size enhances security. Common key sizes range from 2048 to 4096 bits.

Applications of RSA

RSA is extensively used for secure data transmission, digital signatures, and establishing secure SSL/TLS connections. It serves as a foundational component in various security protocols and is integral to Public Key Infrastructure (PKI) implementations.

DSA (Digital Signature Algorithm)

Overview of DSA

The Digital Signature Algorithm (DSA) is a standard for digital signatures, developed by the National Institute of Standards and Technology (NIST) in the 1990s. Unlike RSA, which can be used for both encryption and signing, DSA exclusively focuses on generating and verifying digital signatures.

Key Generation

The following steps outline the key generation process for DSA:

1. **Select Prime Numbers**: Choose a large prime number p and a smaller prime q, where q is a divisor of $p-1$. The value of p should be at least 2048 bits and q at least 256 bits.

2. **Generate the Base**: Find a generator g such that $g = h^{(p-1)/q} \mod p$, where h is a randomly selected integer less than p and not congruent to 0 modulo p.

3. **Choose Private Key**: Select a private key x randomly from the range $[1, q-1]$.

4. **Compute Public Key**: Compute the public key $y = g^x \mod p$.

The DSA public key is represented as (p, q, g, y), while the private key is represented as x.

Signing and Verification

The signing process involves creating a unique signature for each message:

1. **Hash the Message**: Calculate the hash $H(m)$ of the message m using a secure hash function like SHA-256.

2. **Generate Signature**: Choose a random integer k from $[1, q-1]$. Compute:

- $r = (g^k \mod p) \mod q$

- $s = (k^{-1} \cdot (H(m) + x \cdot r)) \mod q$

The digital signature is then represented as the pair (r, s).

To verify the signature, the recipient performs the following steps:

1. **Check Signature Validity**: Ensure that r and s are in the range $[0, q]$.

2. **Calculate the Hash**: Hash the received message m to get $H(m)$.

3. **Compute Verification Values**:

   - $w = s^{-1} \mod q$

   - $u_1 = (H(m) \cdot w) \mod q$

   - $u_2 = (r \cdot w) \mod q$

   - Calculate $V = ((g^{u_1} \cdot y^{u_2}) \mod p) \mod q$

4. **Compare Outputs**: The signature is valid if $V \equiv r \mod q$.

Applications of DSA

DSA is primarily utilized in the Digital Signature Standard (DSS) for digital signing and is embedded within various security protocols. Its efficiency in generating and verifying signatures has made it a crucial part of secure communications.

Diffie-Hellman Key Exchange

Overview of Diffie-Hellman

Diffie-Hellman is a key exchange protocol developed by Whitfield Diffie and Martin Hellman in 1976. It allows two parties to establish a shared secret over an insecure channel, which can then be used for symmetric encryption or other cryptographic purposes.

Key Exchange Process

The steps involved in the Diffie-Hellman key exchange are as follows:

1. **Select Parameters**: Both parties agree

on a large prime number p and a base g, which can be publicly shared.

2. **Individual Secret Selection**: Each party selects a private secret:

   - Alice chooses a secret integer a ($1 < a < p$)

   - Bob chooses a secret integer b ($1 < b < p$)

3. **Public Value Calculation**: Both parties calculate their public values:

   - Alice computes $A = g^a \mod p$

   - Bob computes $B = g^b \mod p$

4. **Public Value Exchange**: Alice sends A to Bob, and Bob sends B to Alice.

5. **Shared Secret Calculation**:

- Alice computes the shared secret $s = B^a \mod p$

- Bob computes the shared secret $s = A^b \mod p$

Both calculations result in the same shared secret $s = g^{ab} \mod p$, which can be used for symmetric key encryption.

Security of Diffie-Hellman

The security of the Diffie-Hellman key exchange lies in the difficulty of the discrete logarithm problem. While an eavesdropper can see A and B, without knowledge of a or b, they cannot feasibly compute the shared secret s.

Applications of Diffie-Hellman

Diffie-Hellman is widely used in various security protocols, such as SSL/TLS for establishing secure web connections. It enables the secure exchange of encryption keys between parties, allowing for secure communication over potentially compromised networks.

Hashing

Overview of Hashing

Hashing is a fundamental cryptographic technique that transforms an input (or message) of any size into a fixed-size string of bytes. The output, known as a hash, is unique to each unique input, making it a powerful tool in ensuring data integrity and authenticity.

Properties of Cryptographic Hash Functions

Effective cryptographic hash functions exhibit several essential properties:

1. **Deterministic**: The same input will always produce the same hash output.

2. **Quick Computation**: It must be fast to compute the hash for any given input.

3. **Pre-image Resistance**: It should be computationally infeasible to reconstruct the original input from its hash output.

4. **Small Changes in Input Produce Drastic Changes in Output**: A small alteration in the input should result in a substantially different hash, a phenomenon known as the avalanche effect.

5. **Collision Resistance**: It must be difficult to find two different inputs that produce the same hash output.

Common Hash Functions

Several hashing algorithms are widely recognized and used in practice, including:

1. **MD5 (Message-Digest Algorithm 5)**: MD5 produces a 128-bit hash value and was commonly used in various applications. However, vulnerabilities have been discovered, making it less secure in modern contexts.

2. **SHA-1 (Secure Hash Algorithm 1)**: SHA-1 generates a 160-bit hash and has also been found to possess vulnerabilities. Its use has been deprecated for many applications.

3. **SHA-2**: This family includes SHA-224, SHA-256, SHA-384, and SHA-512, producing hash outputs of different lengths. SHA-256 is widely used in various security protocols, including Bitcoin and SSL/TLS.

4. **SHA-3**: This standard builds upon the Keccak family of algorithms and represents a newer approach to hashing, providing improved security properties.

Applications of Hashing

Hash functions are prevalent in several applications, including:

- **Data Integrity Verification**: Hashes can be used to check the integrity of files transferred over networks by comparing the hashes before and after transfer.

- **Digital Signatures**: As described earlier, hashing is essential for creating the unique message digest necessary for generating and verifying digital signatures.

- **Password Storage**: Instead of storing plain-text passwords, systems often store hashes of passwords. When users enter their credentials, the system hashes the attempt and compares it to the stored hash.

- **Cryptographic Protocols**: Hash functions play a crucial role in various cryptographic protocols, ensuring data integrity and authenticity.

Asymmetric cryptography has revolutionized the way we secure communications over the internet. With Algorithms like RSA and DSA, we can ensure that messages are confidential and that identities can be verified. The Diffie-Hellman key exchange further facilitates secure key establishment without the need for prior communication of secret keys. Meanwhile, hashing serves as a critical component that underpins many of these operations, ensuring data integrity and authenticity.

As cyber threats continue to evolve, understanding and implementing these cryptographic techniques is essential for maintaining security in our digital communications. The combination of asymmetric encryption, digital signatures, key exchange protocols, and hashing provides a robust framework for modern cybersecurity practices, affirming the importance of ongoing research and development in cryptography.

Chapter 8: Electronic Signatures

Understanding Authenticity and Integrity

In the realm of digital communications, two fundamental pillars that ensure the security and reliability of information are authenticity and integrity. These concepts serve as the backbone of electronic signatures, lending them their power and utility in various applications today.

Authenticity

Authenticity refers to the assurance that the information received is indeed from the claimed sender. In an electronic context, this means that when someone signs a document electronically, it provides definitive proof of their identity. This is particularly crucial in scenarios such as legal agreements, financial transactions, and sensitive communications where knowing the true identity of the sender can prevent fraud and unauthorized actions.

To establish authenticity, several methodologies can be employed. Public key infrastructure (PKI) is a prevalent approach wherein each user has a unique pair of keys: a public key that can be shared openly and a private key that must be kept secure. When a document is signed using a private key, anyone with access to the corresponding public key can confirm the identity of the signer.

Integrity

Integrity, on the other hand, ensures that the content of a message or document has not been altered in transit. When a document is signed electronically, the signature encompasses a hash of the document, which is a fixed-size string that uniquely represents the data. If even a single character in the document changes, the hash will differ, alerting the recipient to potential tampering.

To achieve integrity, cryptographic hash functions are utilized. These functions take an input (or 'message') and produce a fixed-size string of characters, which appears random. Common hash functions include SHA-256 and SHA-3, among others. The immutable nature of the hash is crucial because it allows end parties to validate not only the authenticity of the signature but also the integrity of the signed document.

Implementation of Digital Signatures

The practical application of electronic signatures involves a combination of hardware, software, and cryptographic protocols to ensure secure and efficient signing processes. Below, we outline the steps usually involved in the implementation of digital signatures and the technologies that support them.

Step 1: Key Generation

The first step in implementing digital signatures involves the generation of a pair of cryptographic keys. These keys are produced using complex algorithms that ensure a high level of security and randomness. Popular algorithms for key generation include RSA (Rivest-Shamir-Adleman), DSA (Digital Signature Algorithm), and ECDSA (Elliptic Curve Digital Signature Algorithm).

The security of the digital signature relies on the confidentiality of the private key. If a malicious actor gains access to it, they could impersonate the legitimate user. Therefore, it is essential to adopt robust key management practices, including the use of hardware security modules (HSMs) or secure environments for storing private keys.

Step 2: Signing the Document

Once the keys are generated, the next step is signing a document. This process is typically executed through the following steps:

1. **Hashing the Document**: Prior to signing, the document is hashed using a cryptographic hash function. This produces a unique digest that serves as a representation of the document's content.

2. **Creating the Signature**: The hash is then encrypted with the private key of the signer. This encrypted hash, along with the hash algorithm used, forms the digital signature.

3. **Appending the Signature**: The digital signature is attached to the original document.

In many cases, the signature is embedded within the file itself or provided as a separate piece of data to accompany the document.

Step 3: Sending the Signed Document

After the signature has been applied, the signed document is sent to the recipient. This can be done through various means, such as email, secure file transfer protocols, or through digital transaction platforms designed for document handling.

Step 4: Verification of the Signature

Upon receiving the signed document, the recipient must verify the digital signature to ensure both authenticity and integrity:

1. **Extracting the Signature and Document**: The recipient first extracts the

digital signature and the original document from the received file.

2. **Hashing the Document Again**: Next, the recipient generates a hash of the received document using the same hash function that was used by the signer.

3. **Decrypting the Signature**: The recipient then decrypts the digital signature using the signer's public key. This action will yield the hash value that was created by the signer.

4. **Comparison for Validation**: Finally, the recipient compares the newly generated hash from the document with the decrypted hash obtained from the digital signature. If they match, it confirms that the document is intact (i.e., has not been altered) and that the signature is valid, thereby authenticating the identity of the signer.

Use Cases of Electronic Signatures

The adoption of electronic signatures has seen significant growth across a range of sectors, driven by their efficiency and legal validity. Some common use cases include:

- **Contracts and Agreements**: Businesses leverage electronic signatures to formalize contracts in a time-efficient manner. This includes employment contracts, service agreements, and non-disclosure agreements.

- **Financial Transactions**: Electronic signatures play a critical role in financial services, including loan applications, account opening, and investment agreements. They enhance speed and security while meeting legal requirements.

- **Healthcare**: The healthcare industry employs electronic signatures to manage patient records, consent forms, and prescriptions, ensuring compliance with regulations such as HIPAA (Health Insurance Portability and Accountability Act).

- **Government and Public Sector**: Many governmental agencies now utilize electronic signatures for applications, permits, and approvals, reducing processing times and improving public service efficiency.

Legal Framework

The legal standing of electronic signatures is governed by various national and international regulations. In the United States, the ESIGN Act (Electronic Signatures in Global and National Commerce Act) and UETA (Uniform Electronic Transactions Act) provide the framework for the use of electronic signatures in commerce. Similarly, the European Union's eIDAS Regulation (Electronic Identification and Trust Services) establishes standards for electronic signatures, ensuring their legality and interoperability across member states.

These regulations affirm that electronic signatures are legally equivalent to handwritten signatures, provided that certain conditions are met. Among these are ensuring that the signatory intends to sign the document, the method of signing is reliable, and the recipient can verify the signature's authenticity.

Challenges and Considerations

While electronic signatures offer numerous advantages, their implementation does not come without challenges. A few considerable factors include:

- **Security Risks**: Digital signatures, while generally robust, are not immune to attacks. Phishing attempts, key theft, and unauthorized access are potential threats that organizations must address through stringent cybersecurity measures.

- **Trust Issues**: Trust in electronic signatures is contingent on the integrity of the underlying infrastructure. Issues such as misconfigured systems, reliance on outdated algorithms, or poor key management can undermine the trustworthiness of digital signatures.

- **User Acceptance**: Organizations must facilitate broad user education regarding the use of electronic signatures, as understanding their functionality and legal implications is crucial for adoption.

Future Trends in Electronic Signatures

As technology continues to evolve, the landscape of electronic signatures is set to change further. Some emerging trends include:

- **Integration with Blockchain**: The incorporation of blockchain technology may strengthen the security of electronic signatures by providing tamper-proof storage and audit trails of signed documents.

- **Biometric Authentication**: Integrating biometric measures, such as fingerprints or facial recognition, can bolster the verification process for signers, enhancing trust and security.

- **Artificial Intelligence**: AI could play a role in streamlining signature verification processes, improving efficiency while reducing the prevalence of fraud.

- **Automated Workflow**: The future may see greater automation in the signing process, incorporating smart contracts and other digital tools to facilitate seamless transactions.

Conclusion

In conclusion, electronic signatures represent a pivotal advancement in digital communication and transaction management, promoting both the authenticity of signers and the integrity of signed documents. Their implementation, grounded in cryptographic principles and a robust legal framework, offers organizations and individuals a high level of security and efficiency.

Understanding the concepts of authenticity and integrity is essential for leveraging electronic signatures effectively. As technology progresses, it is vital for stakeholders to remain aware of advancements in this field and the associated challenges to ensure that electronic signatures continue to provide a safe and reliable means of affirming agreement and consent in the digital age.

Chapter 8: Electronic Signatures

Understanding Authenticity and Integrity

In the realm of digital communications, two fundamental pillars that ensure the security and reliability of information are authenticity and integrity. These concepts serve as the backbone of electronic signatures, lending them their power and utility in various applications today.

Authenticity

Authenticity refers to the assurance that the information received is indeed from the claimed sender. In an electronic context, this means that when someone signs a document electronically, it provides definitive proof of their identity. This is particularly crucial in scenarios such as legal agreements, financial transactions, and sensitive communications where knowing the true identity of the sender can prevent fraud and unauthorized actions.

To establish authenticity, several methodologies can be employed. Public key infrastructure (PKI) is a prevalent approach wherein each user has a unique pair of keys: a public key that can be shared openly and a private key that must be kept secure. When a document is signed using a private key, anyone with access to the corresponding public key can confirm the identity of the signer.

Integrity

Integrity, on the other hand, ensures that the content of a message or document has not been altered in transit. When a document is signed electronically, the signature encompasses a hash of the document, which is a fixed-size string that uniquely represents the data. If even a single character in the document changes, the hash will differ, alerting the recipient to potential tampering.

To achieve integrity, cryptographic hash functions are utilized. These functions take an input (or 'message') and produce a fixed-size string of characters, which appears random. Common hash functions include SHA-256 and SHA-3, among others. The immutable nature of the hash is crucial because it allows end parties to validate not only the authenticity of the signature but also the integrity of the signed document.

Implementation of Digital Signatures

The practical application of electronic signatures involves a combination of hardware, software, and cryptographic protocols to ensure secure and efficient signing processes. Below, we outline the steps usually involved in the implementation of digital signatures and the technologies that support them.

Step 1: Key Generation

The first step in implementing digital signatures involves the generation of a pair of cryptographic keys. These keys are produced using complex algorithms that ensure a high level of security and randomness. Popular algorithms for key generation include RSA (Rivest-Shamir-Adleman), DSA (Digital Signature Algorithm), and ECDSA (Elliptic Curve Digital Signature Algorithm).

The security of the digital signature relies on the confidentiality of the private key. If a malicious actor gains access to it, they could impersonate the legitimate user. Therefore, it is essential to adopt robust key management practices, including the use of hardware security modules (HSMs) or secure environments for storing private keys.

Step 2: Signing the Document

Once the keys are generated, the next step is signing a document. This process is typically executed through the following steps:

1. **Hashing the Document**: Prior to signing, the document is hashed using a cryptographic hash function. This produces a unique digest that serves as a representation of the document's content.

2. **Creating the Signature**: The hash is then encrypted with the private key of the signer. This encrypted hash, along with the hash algorithm used, forms the digital signature.

3. **Appending the Signature**: The digital signature is attached to the original document. In many cases, the signature is embedded within the file itself or provided as a separate

piece of data to accompany the document.

Step 3: Sending the Signed Document

After the signature has been applied, the signed document is sent to the recipient. This can be done through various means, such as email, secure file transfer protocols, or through digital transaction platforms designed for document handling.

Step 4: Verification of the Signature

Upon receiving the signed document, the recipient must verify the digital signature to ensure both authenticity and integrity:

1. **Extracting the Signature and Document**: The recipient first extracts the digital signature and the original document from the received file.

2. **Hashing the Document Again**: Next, the recipient generates a hash of the received document using the same hash function that was used by the signer.

3. **Decrypting the Signature**: The recipient then decrypts the digital signature using the signer's public key. This action will yield the hash value that was created by the signer.

4. **Comparison for Validation**: Finally, the recipient compares the newly generated hash from the document with the decrypted hash obtained from the digital signature. If they match, it confirms that the document is intact (i.e., has not been altered) and that the signature is valid, thereby authenticating the identity of the signer.

Use Cases of Electronic Signatures

The adoption of electronic signatures has seen significant growth across a range of sectors, driven by their efficiency and legal validity. Some common use cases include:

- **Contracts and Agreements**: Businesses leverage electronic signatures to formalize contracts in a time-efficient manner. This includes employment contracts, service agreements, and non-disclosure agreements.

- **Financial Transactions**: Electronic signatures play a critical role in financial services, including loan applications, account opening, and investment agreements. They enhance speed and security while meeting legal requirements.

- **Healthcare**: The healthcare industry employs electronic signatures to manage patient records, consent forms, and prescriptions, ensuring compliance with regulations such as HIPAA (Health Insurance

Portability and Accountability Act).

- **Government and Public Sector**: Many governmental agencies now utilize electronic signatures for applications, permits, and approvals, reducing processing times and improving public service efficiency.

Legal Framework

The legal standing of electronic signatures is governed by various national and international regulations. In the United States, the ESIGN Act (Electronic Signatures in Global and National Commerce Act) and UETA (Uniform Electronic Transactions Act) provide the framework for the use of electronic signatures in commerce. Similarly, the European Union's eIDAS Regulation (Electronic Identification and Trust Services) establishes standards for electronic signatures, ensuring their legality and interoperability across member states.

These regulations affirm that electronic signatures are legally equivalent to handwritten signatures, provided that certain conditions are met. Among these are ensuring that the signatory intends to sign the document, the method of signing is reliable, and the recipient can verify the signature's authenticity.

Challenges and Considerations

While electronic signatures offer numerous advantages, their implementation does not come without challenges. A few considerable factors include:

- **Security Risks**: Digital signatures, while generally robust, are not immune to attacks. Phishing attempts, key theft, and unauthorized access are potential threats that organizations must address through stringent cybersecurity measures.

- **Trust Issues**: Trust in electronic signatures is contingent on the integrity of the underlying infrastructure. Issues such as misconfigured systems, reliance on outdated algorithms, or poor key management can undermine the trustworthiness of digital signatures.

- **User Acceptance**: Organizations must facilitate broad user education regarding the use of electronic signatures, as understanding their functionality and legal implications is crucial for adoption.

Future Trends in Electronic Signatures

As technology continues to evolve, the landscape of electronic signatures is set to change further. Some emerging trends include:

- **Integration with Blockchain**: The incorporation of blockchain technology may strengthen the security of electronic signatures by providing tamper-proof storage and audit trails of signed documents.

- **Biometric Authentication**: Integrating biometric measures, such as fingerprints or facial recognition, can bolster the verification process for signers, enhancing trust and security.

- **Artificial Intelligence**: AI could play a role in streamlining signature verification processes, improving efficiency while reducing the prevalence of fraud.

- **Automated Workflow**: The future may see greater automation in the signing process, incorporating smart contracts and other digital tools to facilitate seamless transactions.

In conclusion, electronic signatures represent a pivotal advancement in digital communication and transaction management, promoting both the authenticity of signers and the integrity of signed documents. Their implementation, grounded in cryptographic principles and a robust legal framework, offers organizations and individuals a high level of security and efficiency.

Understanding the concepts of authenticity and integrity is essential for leveraging electronic signatures effectively. As technology progresses, it is vital for stakeholders to remain aware of advancements in this field and the associated challenges to ensure that electronic signatures continue to provide a safe and reliable means of affirming agreement and consent in the digital age.

Chapter 9: Advanced Cryptography

Elliptic Curve Cryptography

1. Fundamentals of Elliptic Curves

Elliptic Curve Cryptography (ECC) is a branch of public-key cryptography that leverages the mathematics of elliptic curves over finite fields. The foundational element in ECC is the elliptic curve itself, defined by a specific equation in the form $y^2 = x^3 + ax + b$, where a and b are coefficients satisfying the condition that the curve has no singular points. This means that the curve does not intersect itself and maintains smoothness, which is essential for the cryptographic properties.

Elliptic curves can be defined over various fields, most notably the real numbers, complex numbers, and finite fields. In cryptography, we are primarily concerned with curves defined over finite fields, particularly those denoted as $\mathbb{F}_p$ (where p is a prime number) or $\mathbb{F}_{2^m}$ (binary fields).

The points on an elliptic curve form an abelian group, which is crucial for ECC. The group operation is defined geometrically: given two points P and Q on the curve, their sum $R = P + Q$ can be found by drawing a line through P and Q to find the third intersection point with the curve; the reflection of this point across the x-axis gives the resulting point R. This addition is defined algebraically and helps establish properties critical for cryptographic protocols.

A significant aspect of ECC is its use of the elliptic curve discrete logarithm problem (ECDLP), which is defined as finding the integer k given points P and Q such that $Q = kP$. The hardness of this problem forms the backbone of the security offered by

ECC.

2. Advantages over Traditional Algorithms

Elliptic Curve Cryptography provides several notable advantages over traditional public-key algorithms such as RSA and DSA:

a. Smaller Key Size

One of the most compelling benefits of ECC is that it offers equivalent security with significantly smaller key sizes. For instance, a 256-bit key in ECC can provide security comparable to a 3072-bit key in RSA. This smaller key size leads to less computational overhead, faster computations, and reduced storage requirements.

b. Efficiency

Due to the smaller key sizes, ECC is generally more efficient in terms of both processing power and bandwidth usage. This aspect is particularly important in resource-constrained environments such as mobile devices and embedded systems, where power and processing capabilities might be limited.

c. Enhanced Security

Elliptic curves have a structure that makes them robust against certain types of attacks that affect traditional algorithms. For example, advancements in quantum computing are expected to challenge RSA and DSA systems due to Shor's algorithm; however, ECC can still provide a feasible level of security as the quantum threat is less straightforward with ECDLP.

d. Scalability

As security requirements evolve, the scalability of ECC facilitates easier adjustments. Users can migrate to longer keys without necessitating complete system overhauls, which would be more cumbersome in traditional systems.

3. Applications in Mobile Systems and IoT

The integration of ECC into mobile systems and Internet of Things (IoT) environments has been driven by its optimized performance and robustness. Here are several key areas where ECC is utilized:

a. Secure Communications

ECC is widely used in protocols such as Secure Socket Layer (SSL)/Transport Layer

Security (TLS), which can secure communications over networks. These protocols ensure secure connections between clients and servers, tackling issues such as data integrity, confidentiality, and authentication—critical in mobile commerce and IoT communications.

b. Authentication

Various authentication protocols leverage ECC to verify identities while maintaining security in communication. ECC-based digital signatures (like ECDSA) provide a more efficient authentication process, often implemented in mobile banking and financial applications to enable quick yet secure transactions.

c. Encryption in Low-Power Devices

IoT devices, which often operate with limited

computational capability and battery life, greatly benefit from ECC's efficiency. ECC algorithms facilitate secure communications without excessively draining resources, allowing devices to function longer while maintaining robust security.

d. Blockchain and Cryptocurrencies

ECC has found a strong footing in blockchain technology and cryptocurrency systems. Bitcoin, for example, employs ECDSA for signing transactions, benefiting from ECC's compact key sizes to reduce network congestion and storage demands. This application showcases ECC's versatility and robustness in ensuring the integrity and authenticity of digital transactions across decentralized platforms.

e. Secure Identification Systems

In identity management, ECC provides an effective means of securing user identities and access control systems. The efficiency and high-security promise make it ideal for implementing secure access systems in mobile applications, replacing traditional password-based systems with ECC-based public-private key pairs.

4. Conclusion

Elliptic Curve Cryptography represents a significant advancement in cryptographic technology, combining mathematical elegance with practical efficiency. Its advantages over traditional algorithms make it a favorable choice in modern applications, especially in mobile computing and the ever-growing realm of IoT. As the digital landscape continues to evolve, with increasing demands for security and privacy, ECC is poised to play a pivotal role in shaping the way we secure communications and transactions in all facets of technology.

As we embrace ECC, it is essential to remain aware of best practices in implementing these systems strategically. Ensuring that proper elliptic curves are selected (following guidelines such as those provided by organizations like NIST) and managing resources adequately will allow the full potential of ECC to be realized across various applications, safeguarding our digital future.

In the subsequent chapters, we will explore the practical implementation challenges of ECC, delve into advanced cryptographic protocols leveraging elliptic curves, and discuss evolving trends in the cryptographic landscape driven by ongoing research and emerging security threats.

Chapter 10: Post-Quantum Cryptography

Introduction to Quantum Threats

The advent of quantum computing poses significant challenges to current cryptographic systems, primarily due to the computational power these machines can harness. Unlike classical computers, which operate on bits that must be either 0 or 1, quantum computers use quantum bits, or qubits. These qubits can exist in multiple states simultaneously thanks to the principle of superposition, allowing quantum computers to solve certain problems exponentially faster than their classical counterparts.

The most renowned quantum algorithm that threatens existing cryptographic systems is Shor's algorithm. Shor's algorithm can factor large integers efficiently, fundamentally undermining the security of widely used public key cryptosystems, such as RSA and

ECC (Elliptic Curve Cryptography). The ability of quantum computers to break these systems raises a pressing concern in cybersecurity, necessitating the development of algorithms that can withstand quantum computational capabilities.

Quantum Threats to Cryptography

1. Public Key Infrastructure (PKI)

Public key cryptography relies on mathematical problems believed to be hard to solve. RSA, for instance, is based on the difficulty of factoring the product of two large prime numbers. With Shor's algorithm, a sufficiently powerful quantum computer could factor these large integers in polynomial time, rendering RSA obsolete. Similarly, ECC relies on the difficulty of the Elliptic Curve Discrete Logarithm Problem (ECDLP), which can also be solved quickly by quantum computers using Shor's algorithm.

2. Symmetric Key Cryptography

While symmetric key algorithms, such as AES (Advanced Encryption Standard), are not directly vulnerable to Shor's algorithm, they are still affected by the advent of quantum computing. Grover's algorithm provides a quadratic speedup for searching through unsorted databases, effectively halving the bit security. For instance, a 128-bit key in AES would provide roughly 2^{64} security against a quantum adversary, which is considered feasible for future quantum computers. As a mitigating strategy, symmetric key lengths need to be increased. For example, it is recommended to use a minimum of 256 bits for AES to ensure security in a post-quantum world.

3. Digital Signatures

Digital signatures play a crucial role in authenticating entities and ensuring data integrity. Most digital signature schemes, including those based on RSA, DSA (Digital Signature Algorithm), and ECDSA (Elliptic Curve Digital Signature Algorithm), are also susceptible to quantum attacks through Shor's algorithm. Thus, there is an immediate need for post-quantum secure signing mechanisms that are resilient against the capabilities of quantum machines.

Post-Quantum Cryptographic Algorithms

The critical need for cryptography that can withstand the capabilities of quantum computers has led to extensive research in the domain of post-quantum cryptography. The aim is to develop new cryptographic algorithms based on mathematical structures that are believed to be secure against quantum attacks. Some of these structures include lattice problems, hash functions, multivariate polynomials, and code-based systems.

1. Lattice-Based Cryptography

Lattice-based cryptographic algorithms are a prominent candidate for post-quantum cryptography. These algorithms derive their security from the hardness of solving certain lattice problems, such as the Shortest Vector Problem (SVP) and the Learning With Errors (LWE) problem.

- **Advantages**: Lattice-based schemes are known for their efficiency and the ability to reduce the complexity of quantum attacks, making them suitable for a wide range of applications, including encryption, digital signatures, and key exchange.

- **Example Algorithms**: Two notable lattice-based schemes include NTRU (a public key encryption scheme) and the FrodoKEM (a key exchange mechanism).

2. Code-Based Cryptography

Code-based cryptography relies on the complexity of decoding a random linear code. The McEliece cryptosystem, developed in the 1970s, is among the most famous code-based schemes. It utilizes error-correcting codes to secure data.

- **Security**: The difficulty of certain decoding problems provides a solid foundation for security against quantum attacks. McEliece is particularly attractive due to its long-standing track record of resilience over several decades.

- **Trade-offs**: While the McEliece cryptosystem is known for its security, it has larger public key sizes compared to other contemporary systems, which can pose challenges in practical applications.

3. Multivariate Polynomial Cryptography

Multivariate public key cryptography is based on the intractability of solving systems of multivariate polynomial equations over finite fields. This method is particularly useful for constructing digital signature schemes.

- **Notable Systems**: The Rainbow signature scheme is one of the most well-known multivariate schemes and has been submitted to the NIST post-quantum cryptography project for standardization.

- **Security**: Its security is based on the hard problem of finding a solution to random multivariate equations, which is believed to be resistant to both classical and quantum attacks.

4. Hash-Based Cryptography

Hash-based cryptography utilizes the security of cryptographic hash functions to build secure signature schemes. One of the most developed schemes in this category is the XMSS (eXtended Merkle Signature Scheme), which offers secure, stateful signatures.

- **Efficiency**: Hash-based signatures can be efficient and are applicable for many scenarios, although their statefulness—where the signer cannot reuse the same key for multiple signatures—needs to be carefully managed.

5. Other Considerations

As more research emerges in the field of post-quantum cryptography, it is essential to consider additional criteria such as:

- **Speed and Efficiency**: The algorithms must be computationally efficient and practical for real-world applications.

- **Implementation Security**: Resistance to side-channel attacks and other implementation vulnerabilities is crucial.

- **Standardization**: Initiatives such as the NIST Post-Quantum Cryptography Standardization Project are working to evaluate and standardize post-quantum algorithms, which will facilitate their adoption and use.

Conclusion: Preparing for the Post-Quantum Era

The transition to post-quantum cryptography will not happen overnight; it requires careful planning, testing, and validation to ensure that new systems are effective and secure. Organizations must start preparing for this shift by adopting hybrid cryptographic schemes that implement both classical and post-quantum algorithms in parallel. This will allow for a gradual transition while maintaining security against existing quantum threats.

While quantum computers may have the potential to disrupt conventional cryptographic systems, they also serve as a catalyst for innovation in cryptography. By fostering research and the development of quantum-resistant algorithms, the field is now moving toward a more secure digital landscape that can withstand the challenges posed by the quantum age. The timeline for quantum computing's practical realization remains uncertain, but proactive measures will help in fortifying cryptographic systems in anticipation of the changing technological landscape.

Chapter 11: Homomorphic Encryption

Concept of Computing on Encrypted Data

Homomorphic encryption is a fascinating field in cryptography that allows computations to be performed on ciphertexts, producing an encrypted result that, when decrypted, matches the result of operations performed on the plaintext. This revolutionary concept opens up new avenues for data security, privacy, and computing, particularly in an era where data is constantly being collected and analyzed.

The basic idea of homomorphic encryption can be traced back to the desire to perform operations on sensitive data without ever exposing the data itself. Traditional encryption methods require data to be decrypted before any operations can be performed. In contrast, homomorphic encryption eliminates the need to reveal the original data, allowing computations to be carried out on encrypted values.

There are three primary types of homomorphic encryption:

1. **Partially Homomorphic Encryption (PHE)**: This type supports a limited number of operations (either addition or multiplication) on encrypted data. For example, RSA is partially homomorphic concerning multiplication, while the Paillier system is homomorphic concerning addition.

2. **Somewhat Homomorphic Encryption (SHE)**: This kind allows a bounded number of both additions and multiplications but is limited in the complexity of computations that can be performed. SHE schemes are typically non-relativistic, meaning they cannot support arbitrarily complex operations indefinitely.

3. **Fully Homomorphic Encryption (FHE)**: As the most advanced form, FHE supports an unlimited number of both additions and multiplications on encrypted data. It allows for arbitrary computations to be performed without ever needing to decrypt the underlying data.

The ability to perform computations on encrypted data is primarily accomplished through a careful engineering of mathematical structures and algorithms. Each homomorphic encryption scheme employs different mathematical techniques to maintain the ciphertext representation while enabling specific operations.

Applications of Homomorphic Encryption

Homomorphic encryption stands to make

significant contributions across various sectors and applications. Its implications extend into fields such as cloud computing, healthcare, finance, and privacy-preserving machine learning. Below are a few key applications:

1. **Cloud Computing**: As businesses increasingly rely on cloud services for data storage and processing, concerns regarding data privacy escalate. Homomorphic encryption allows users to store their sensitive data in the cloud while still being able to perform computations without decrypting the data, ensuring maximum privacy. For example, a user could encrypt medical records and allow a cloud-based application to analyze them for patterns without exposing the underlying data.

2. **Healthcare**: In healthcare, patient data confidentiality is paramount. Homomorphic encryption allows researchers to perform statistical analysis on encrypted clinical data without accessing sensitive patient

information. This enables collaborative research across institutions while mitigating privacy risks.

3. **Finance**: Financial institutions can leverage homomorphic encryption to process encrypted transactions, perform risk assessment, and compute credit scores without exposing sensitive customer data. This added layer of security can be critical in maintaining customer trust and ensuring regulatory compliance.

4. **Privacy-Preserving Machine Learning**: Machine learning algorithms typically require access to large datasets, which can include sensitive information. Using homomorphic encryption, researchers can train machine learning models on encrypted data, ensuring that sensitive data does not need to be revealed during the training process. This capability opens new possibilities for developing predictive models while maintaining data privacy.

5. **Voting Systems**: Secure electronic voting systems can benefit from homomorphic encryption by allowing votes to be cast as encrypted data. The voting process could be executed in such a way that even while counting the votes, the individual ballots remain confidential, with the final result being verifiable without revealing individual preferences.

6. **Data Sovereignty**: As regulations around data privacy increase, such as the GDPR in Europe, homomorphic encryption provides a method to analyze and utilize data while complying with legal guidelines. Organizations can maintain control over their encrypted data even if processed off-site.

Challenges of Homomorphic Encryption

Despite its promising applications,

homomorphic encryption faces several challenges that must be addressed for it to become a mainstream solution.

1. **Performance Overhead**: One of the significant challenges of homomorphic encryption is its computational efficiency. The performance of homomorphic operations is considerably lower than their plaintext counterparts. For example, the time complexity for performing operations on encrypted data can be several orders of magnitude slower than on unencrypted data. This overhead can limit the practical usability of homomorphic encryption, especially in time-sensitive applications.

2. **Large Ciphertext Size**: Homomorphic encryption schemes tend to produce ciphertexts that are significantly larger than the original data. This increase in size results from the complex mathematical structures used to support the homomorphic properties. The larger the ciphertext, the more storage and

bandwidth are required for transmission, which can hinder the scalability of systems employing homomorphic encryption.

3. **Key Management**: The management of keys in a homomorphic encryption system can become complex, especially when different operations or users require different access rights. Ensuring that the keys remain secure while being managed and distributed properly is a critical aspect that must be carefully designed.

4. **Limited Functionality**: While fully homomorphic encryption theoretically allows for arbitrary computation, the practical implementations are often limited in the types of operations that can efficiently be executed. Certain complex functions and algorithms may not yet be compatible with existing homomorphic schemes, which can limit their applicability.

5. **Standardization and Adoption**: There is an urgent need for standardized protocols and practices for implementing homomorphic encryption. The lack of established standards can create barriers for organizations looking to adopt this technology, as they may be uncertain about best practices, interoperability, and compliance with regulations.

6. **Resistance to Advanced Attacks**: As the field of cryptography evolves and computational capabilities increase, homomorphic encryption schemes must remain robust against emerging attack vectors. Ongoing research is essential to anticipate and mitigate potential vulnerabilities.

7. **User Education and Usability**: For homomorphic encryption to be widely adopted, users must be educated on its use and implications. This includes understanding encryption processes, key management, and system usability. Development of user-

friendly interfaces and support systems is essential in encouraging broader implementation.

Homomorphic encryption represents a significant breakthrough in the ongoing quest for data privacy and security in an increasingly interconnected world. By allowing computations to be performed on encrypted data without exposing it, this cryptographic technique has the potential to revolutionize how sensitive information is processed across various industries.

Despite its challenges, ongoing research and development in the field promise to address many of these limitations, paving the way for enhanced performance, usability, and practical applications. As organizations and individuals become more conscious of privacy concerns and data protection laws, the role of homomorphic encryption is likely to become more pronounced.

In sum, the future of homomorphic encryption seems promising, with the potential to offer innovative solutions to the pressing challenges of data security, privacy, and compliance in the digital age. As technology advances, the continued exploration of this fascinating area of cryptography will yield significant benefits for society as a whole.

Chapter 12: Practical Implementation of Cryptography

In this chapter, we will explore the practical aspects of cryptography, focusing on various libraries and tools that are essential for implementing cryptographic functions securely and efficiently. We will delve into three prominent libraries: OpenSSL, Bouncy Castle, and Libsodium. Additionally, we will cover the important topic of hashing, discussing various algorithms, their use cases, and how they integrate with these libraries.

12.1 Introduction to Cryptographic Libraries

Cryptographic libraries provide developers with robust and tested APIs to work with complex cryptographic algorithms without the need to implement them from scratch. By using established libraries, developers can ensure that they are utilizing industry-standard practices, benefiting from optimizations, and reducing the risk of introducing vulnerabilities.

In this section, we will look into three widely-used cryptographic libraries:

- OpenSSL

- Bouncy Castle

- Libsodium

Each library has its strengths, weaknesses, and specific areas of use, which we will discuss in detail.

12.1.1 OpenSSL

OpenSSL is one of the most popular and

widely used libraries for implementing cryptographic functions. It provides a robust set of tools for SSL/TLS protocols and a comprehensive suite of cryptographic algorithms. OpenSSL is written in C and supports a wide variety of platforms, which makes it a staple in both server-side and client-side cryptographic applications.

Features and Capabilities

1. **SSL/TLS Support**: OpenSSL is best known for its SSL/TLS capabilities, allowing developers to implement secure communications over the internet. This is crucial for any application that transmits sensitive data.

2. **Cryptographic Algorithms**: OpenSSL supports a broad range of algorithms, including symmetric ciphers (AES, DES, etc.), asymmetric ciphers (RSA, DSA, ECC), hashing functions (SHA-256, SHA-512), and

digital signatures.

3. **Performance**: OpenSSL is highly optimized for performance, making it suitable for high-load server environments where speed is critical.

4. **Command Line Tool**: OpenSSL also includes a command line tool that allows users to perform various cryptographic operations, making it useful for testing and debugging cryptographic implementations.

Example of Usage

Here is a brief example of how you can use OpenSSL to generate an RSA key pair and encrypt/decrypt a message.

```bash
```

```
# Generate an RSA private key

openssl genpkey -algorithm RSA -out
private_key.pem -pkeyopt
rsa_keygen_bits:2048


# Extract the public key

openssl rsa -pubout -in private_key.pem -out
public_key.pem


# Encrypt a message using the public key

echo "Hello, World!" | openssl rsautl -encrypt
-inkey public_key.pem -pubin -out
encrypted_message.bin


# Decrypt the message using the private key

openssl rsautl -decrypt -in
encrypted_message.bin -inkey
private_key.pem

```
```
```

12.1.2 Bouncy Castle

Bouncy Castle is a lightweight cryptography API for Java and C#. It offers a wide range of cryptographic operations, including encryption, hashing, and digital signatures. The design philosophy behind Bouncy Castle emphasizes simplicity and usability, which makes it a favorite among Java developers.

Features and Capabilities

1. **Comprehensive API**: Bouncy Castle provides a comprehensive set of APIs for both Java and C#, allowing developers to implement a wide variety of cryptographic operations.

2. **Support for Multiple Algorithms**: Similar to OpenSSL, Bouncy Castle supports a wide range of algorithms and protocols, including various symmetric and asymmetric

encryption algorithms, hashing functions, and more.

3. **Lightweight Design**: Bouncy Castle is designed to be lightweight, making it suitable for environments with limited resources.

4. **Extensibility**: The library is highly extensible, allowing developers to add their own cryptographic algorithms or modify existing ones.

Example of Usage

Here's a simple example of using Bouncy Castle to encrypt and decrypt a message using AES in Java.

```java
import
```

```java
org.bouncycastle.jce.provider.BouncyCastlePr
ovider;

import javax.crypto.Cipher;

import javax.crypto.KeyGenerator;

import javax.crypto.SecretKey;


import java.security.Security;


public class AESExample {

    public static void main(String[] args)
throws Exception {

        Security.addProvider(new
BouncyCastleProvider());


        // Generate an AES key

        KeyGenerator keyGen =
KeyGenerator.getInstance("AES");

        keyGen.init(128); // Key size

        SecretKey secretKey =
```

```java
keyGen.generateKey();

// Create a Cipher for AES encryption
Cipher cipher =
Cipher.getInstance("AES/GCM/NoPadding");

// Encrypt the message
cipher.init(Cipher.ENCRYPT_MODE,
secretKey);
byte[] encryptedData =
cipher.doFinal("Hello, World!".getBytes());

// Decrypt the message
cipher.init(Cipher.DECRYPT_MODE,
secretKey, cipher.getParameters());
byte[] decryptedData =
cipher.doFinal(encryptedData);

System.out.println(new
```

```
String(decryptedData));

    }

}

```
```

12.1.3 Libsodium

Libsodium is a modern, easy-to-use, and
robust library designed for encryption,
decryption, signatures, password hashing, and
cryptographic hashing. Its design emphasizes
usability and safety, making it suitable for
developers who may not be cryptographic
experts.

Features and Capabilities

1. **Simplicity**: Libsodium is designed to
be easy to use, which lowers the barrier for
developers looking to implement
```

cryptography in their applications.

2. **Modern Cryptographic Techniques**:
Libsodium implements state-of-the-art
authentication and encryption algorithms,
avoiding outdated or insecure methods.

3. **Password Hashing**: One of its notable
features is its support for secure password
hashing, which is crucial for applications
dealing with user credentials.

4. **Clear Documentation**: Libsodium is
well-documented and offers a clear API,
making it easier for developers to implement
cryptographic features without extensive
cryptographic knowledge.

Example of Usage

Here is an example of using Libsodium in

Python to encrypt and decrypt a message:

```python
import nacl.secret
import nacl.utils

# Generate a random encryption key
key = nacl.utils.random(nacl.secret.SecretBox.KEY_SIZE)

# Create a SecretBox with the key
box = nacl.secret.SecretBox(key)

# Encrypt the message
message = b"Hello, World!"
encrypted = box.encrypt(message)
```

```
# Decrypt the message

decrypted = box.decrypt(encrypted)


print(decrypted.decode())
```

12.2 Hashing

Hashing is a fundamental cryptographic process used to convert input data of any size into a fixed-size string of characters, which is typically a digest. This process is irreversible, meaning you cannot recover the original data from the hash output. Hashing is widely used in various applications, including data integrity verification, password storage, and digital signatures.

12.2.1 Cryptographic Hash Functions

A good cryptographic hash function has several important properties:

1. **Deterministic**: The same input will always produce the same output.

2. **Fast to Compute**: It should be quick to calculate the hash for any given input.

3. **Pre-image Resistance**: It should be infeasible to generate the original input given its hash.

4. **Small Changes in Input Alter the Output**: A small change in the input should produce a significantly different hash.

5. **Collision Resistant**: It should be difficult to find two distinct inputs that produce the same hash.

Popular cryptographic hash functions include:

- **SHA-256** and **SHA-512**: Part of the SHA-2 family, widely used in various security protocols, including SSL/TLS and cryptocurrencies.

- **SHA-3**: The latest member of the Secure Hash Algorithm family, designed to enhance security and performance.

- **BLAKE2**: A fast cryptographic hash function that provides a good balance between security and speed.

12.2.2 Example of Hashing with OpenSSL and Bouncy Castle

Here's how you would hash a string using SHA-256 with OpenSSL and Bouncy Castle.

OpenSSL Example:

```bash
echo -n "Hello, World!" | openssl dgst -sha256
```

Bouncy Castle Example (Java):

```java
import
org.bouncycastle.jce.provider.BouncyCastlePr
ovider;

import java.security.MessageDigest;

import java.security.Security;

public class HashExample {

    public static void main(String[] args)
throws Exception {

        Security.addProvider(new
BouncyCastleProvider());

        String input = "Hello, World!";

        MessageDigest digest =
```

```
MessageDigest.getInstance("SHA-256");

     byte[] hash =
digest.digest(input.getBytes());


     // Print the hex representation of the hash

     StringBuilder hexString = new
StringBuilder();

     for (byte b : hash) {

          String hex = Integer.toHexString(0xff
& b);

          if (hex.length() == 1)
hexString.append('0');

          hexString.append(hex);

     }

     System.out.println(hexString.toString());

  }

}
```
```
```

In this chapter, we have delved into the practical implementation of cryptographic principles using established libraries such as OpenSSL, Bouncy Castle, and Libsodium. Each library has its strengths suited to various applications, providing essential tools for encryption, digital signatures, and secure data handling.

Additionally, we highlighted the importance of hashing in securing data integrity and user credentials. Understanding how to leverage these libraries effectively is crucial for developers looking to implement cryptographic functions securely and efficiently.

As the landscape of cryptography continues to evolve, it is imperative for developers to stay updated with best practices and ongoing developments in cryptographic techniques to ensure that their applications remain secure against emerging threats.

Chapter 13: Developing Cryptographic Applications

In the realm of cybersecurity, cryptography plays a pivotal role in securing communication, protecting sensitive data, and ensuring privacy in an increasingly interconnected world. This chapter delves deeper into the development of cryptographic applications by exploring best practices for implementing cryptographic algorithms, along with practical examples that illustrate these concepts effectively.

Best Practices for Cryptography

When developing cryptographic applications, adhering to best practices is essential. These practices help ensure that your application is secure, resistant to common attacks, and compliant with established standards. Below are several guidelines that should be followed:

1. Use Established Cryptographic Standards

Cryptographic algorithms should be chosen based on established standards and should be widely recognized and vetted by the cryptographic community. Standards such as AES (Advanced Encryption Standard) for symmetric encryption, RSA (Rivest–Shamir–Adleman) for asymmetric encryption, and SHA (Secure Hash Algorithm) for hashing should be prioritized.

Avoid creating custom algorithms, as the security of such implementations is often untested and likely weaker than standard algorithms.

2. Proper Key Management

The security of cryptographic systems heavily relies on the security of keys. Effective key management strategies include:

- **Key Generation**: Use a secure random number generator to create cryptographic keys. Libraries such as OpenSSL or those in languages like Python (e.g., `secrets` module) offer secure random functions.

- **Key Storage**: Store cryptographic keys in secure locations. Consider using hardware security modules (HSMs) or key management services (KMS) offered by cloud providers (AWS KMS, Azure Key Vault).

- **Key Rotation**: Regularly rotate cryptographic keys to minimize the impact of a potential compromise. Automate key rotation where possible to enhance security further.

- **Key Destruction**: Ensure that keys are properly destroyed when they are no longer needed, preventing unauthorized reuse.

3. Limit Data Exposure

Only encrypt and decrypt the data that is necessary. Limit the amount of data exposed by adhering to the principle of least privilege in your applications. Avoid transmitting sensitive data such as passwords or personal information unless absolutely necessary, and consider using tokenization to obfuscate sensitive data in transit or at rest.

4. Use Strong Cryptographic Parameters

When configuring cryptographic algorithms, use strong parameters. For instance:

- **AES**: Use a key length of at least 256 bits.

- **RSA**: Use a key length of at least 2048 bits.

- **DH** (Diffie-Hellman): Use a group size of at least 2048 bits.

5. Implement Secure Protocols

Whenever possible, rely on secure protocols that incorporate cryptographic protections, such as TLS (Transport Layer Security) for network communication. Ensure that the protocol is correctly implemented and configured to prevent vulnerabilities like Man-in-the-Middle (MitM) attacks.

6. Protect Against Common Attacks

Cryptographic applications should be designed to be resilient against known attacks, including:

- **Replay Attacks**: Implement nonces or

timestamps to ensure that each request is unique.

- **Timing Attacks**: Use constant-time algorithms to prevent attackers from gaining insights based on execution time.

- **Padding Oracle Attacks**: Use padding schemes that are resilient, such as OAEP for RSA or PKCS#7 for symmetric encryption.

7. Regular Updates and Audits

Cryptographic libraries and algorithms can become vulnerable over time due to advancements in computational power and new attacks. Regularly update your cryptographic libraries to the latest versions and conduct security audits of your cryptographic implementations.

8. Educate and Train Developers

Developers should be well-versed in cryptographic principles and the importance of security in application development. Providing training and establishing a culture of security awareness can help mitigate risks associated with human error.

9. Code Reviews and Security Testing

Implement rigorous code reviews to identify potential vulnerabilities in cryptographic code. Additionally, utilize static and dynamic analysis tools to test for security issues. Penetration testing should also be conducted to simulate attacks and evaluate the resistance of your application against potential vulnerabilities.

Practical Implementation Examples

In this section, we will examine practical implementations of cryptographic methods in various programming environments. The following examples utilize well-known libraries that provide robust support for handling cryptography.

Example 1: Symmetric Encryption with AES in Python

This example demonstrates how to perform symmetric encryption using AES in the Python programming language. We will leverage the `Cryptography` library for this purpose.

```python
from cryptography.hazmat.backends import default_backend

from cryptography.hazmat.primitives.ciphers import Cipher, algorithms, modes
```

```python
import os

import base64


def encrypt_aes(key, plaintext):

    # Generate a random initialization vector
(IV)

    iv = os.urandom(16)  # AES block size is
16 bytes

    cipher = Cipher(algorithms.AES(key),
modes.CFB(iv), backend=default_backend())

    encryptor = cipher.encryptor()

    ciphertext =
encryptor.update(plaintext.encode()) +
encryptor.finalize()

    return base64.b64encode(iv +
ciphertext).decode('utf-8')


def decrypt_aes(key, encrypted_text):

    # Decode the base64 encoded text
```

```python
    encrypted_bytes =
base64.b64decode(encrypted_text)

    iv = encrypted_bytes[:16]  # Extract the IV
from the beginning

    ciphertext = encrypted_bytes[16:]

    cipher = Cipher(algorithms.AES(key),
modes.CFB(iv), backend=default_backend())

    decryptor = cipher.decryptor()

    plaintext = decryptor.update(ciphertext) +
decryptor.finalize()

    return plaintext.decode('utf-8')


# Example usage

key = os.urandom(32)  # Generate a random
256-bit key

plaintext = "This is a secret message."

encrypted_text = encrypt_aes(key, plaintext)

print(f"Encrypted: {encrypted_text}")
```

```
decrypted_text = decrypt_aes(key,
encrypted_text)

print(f"Decrypted: {decrypted_text}")
```

Explanation:

- This example begins by defining functions for encryption and decryption using AES.

- A random IV is generated for each encryption to ensure that the same plaintext produces different ciphertexts.

- The ciphertext and the IV are concatenated, base64 encoded, and returned as the output of the encryption function.

- The decryption function extracts the IV from the first 16 bytes of the input and decrypts the remaining data.

Example 2: Asymmetric Encryption with RSA in Java

Java provides the `java.security` library, which can be utilized for RSA encryption and decryption.

```java
import java.security.*;

import javax.crypto.Cipher;

import java.util.Base64;


public class RSAExample {

    private static final String ALGORITHM = "RSA";


    public static String encrypt(String plaintext, PublicKey publicKey) throws Exception {

        Cipher cipher = Cipher.getInstance(ALGORITHM);

        cipher.init(Cipher.ENCRYPT_MODE,
```

```java
publicKey);

    byte[] encryptedBytes =
cipher.doFinal(plaintext.getBytes());

    return
Base64.getEncoder().encodeToString(encrypt
edBytes);

    }


    public static String decrypt(String
encryptedText, PrivateKey privateKey)
throws Exception {

    Cipher cipher =
Cipher.getInstance(ALGORITHM);

        cipher.init(Cipher.DECRYPT_MODE,
privateKey);

        byte[] decryptedBytes =
Base64.getDecoder().decode(encryptedText);

        return new
String(cipher.doFinal(decryptedBytes));

    }
```

```java
    public static void main(String[] args)
throws Exception {

    // Generate RSA key pair

    KeyPairGenerator keyGen =
KeyPairGenerator.getInstance(ALGORITHM
);

    keyGen.initialize(2048); // Key size of
2048 bits

    KeyPair keyPair =
keyGen.generateKeyPair();

    PublicKey publicKey =
keyPair.getPublic();

    PrivateKey privateKey =
keyPair.getPrivate();


    String plaintext = "This is a secret
message.";

    String encryptedText = encrypt(plaintext,
publicKey);
```

```
    System.out.println("Encrypted: " +
encryptedText);


    String decryptedText =
decrypt(encryptedText, privateKey);

    System.out.println("Decrypted: " +
decryptedText);

  }

}
```
```

### Explanation:


- The `RSAExample` class demonstrates simple RSA encryption and decryption.

- RSA keys are generated using the `KeyPairGenerator` class, specifying a key size of 2048 bits for security.

- The `encrypt` and `decrypt` methods utilize a `Cipher` instance to perform encryption and
```

decryption using RSA.

- The program prints both the encrypted and decrypted text.

Example 3: Hashing with SHA-256 in JavaScript

For web applications, JavaScript can be used to create SHA-256 hashes via the Web Crypto API.

```javascript
async function hashMessage(message) {
    const encoder = new TextEncoder();
    const data = encoder.encode(message);

    const hash = await crypto.subtle.digest('SHA-256', data);
    return Array.from(new
```

```
Uint8Array(hash)).map(b => ('00' +
b.toString(16)).slice(-2)).join('');

}


hashMessage("This is a secret message.")

  .then(hash => {

    console.log("SHA-256 Hash:", hash);

  });
```
```

### Explanation:


- This example shows how to use the Web
Crypto API to hash a message.

- The `hashMessage` function takes a string
message, encodes it to a `Uint8Array`, and
hashes it using the SHA-256 algorithm.

- The resulting hash is formatted as a
hexadecimal string for easy readability.
```

Conclusion

The development of secure cryptographic applications is a multi-faceted and ever-evolving discipline that requires a strong understanding of cryptographic principles, best practices, and real-world implementations. By adhering to established standards, practicing effective key management, protecting against known attacks, and relying on secure protocols, developers can create robust applications that withstand modern threats.

The practical examples provided in Python, Java, and JavaScript serve to illuminate the core principles of cryptography and enable developers to integrate secure cryptographic practices into their applications successfully. As the cybersecurity landscape continues to change, it is essential that developers remain vigilant, continuously learning and adapting to new threats and technological advancements. This commitment to security will not only protect sensitive information but also foster trust in the systems we build and use every day.

Chapter 14: Security and Vulnerabilities

In the realm of cybersecurity, encryption plays a pivotal role in safeguarding sensitive information. However, despite its effectiveness, cryptographic systems are not immune to various forms of attacks. This chapter will delve into common attacks on cryptography, specifically focusing on brute force attacks, side-channel attacks, and fault-based attacks. Understanding these vulnerabilities is crucial for developing robust encryption systems and ensuring the security of information in a diverse range of applications.

14.1 Brute Force Attacks

Brute force attacks are a straightforward yet powerful method used by attackers to gain access to encrypted data. This type of attack relies on the exhaustive trial-and-error process of guessing the password or key used to encrypt the information. The key aspect of brute force attacks is that they do not exploit any weakness in the cryptographic algorithm itself; instead, they depend solely on the weakness of the key or password used for encryption.

14.1.1 Mechanics of Brute Force Attacks

In a brute force attack, the attacker systematically tries every possible combination of characters until the correct one is found. The success of this method is largely contingent on two factors: the length of the key and the complexity of the characters used.

For instance, a four-digit numeric PIN has 10,000 possible combinations (from 0000 to 9999). In contrast, an eight-character password that includes uppercase letters, lowercase letters, numbers, and special characters can have a staggering 6.1 trillion possible combinations. The time required to execute a brute force attack increases exponentially with the length and complexity of the key.

14.1.2 Time Complexity

The time to crack a key using brute force is dictated by the formula:

$$T = N^k$$

Where:

- T = Total possible combinations

- N = Number of possible characters (e.g., 26 letters for a lowercase alphabet, 62 for both upper and lower case, etc.)

- k = Length of the key

As the values of N and k increase, the

time required to discover the key escalates dramatically. Hence, using longer and more complex keys is critical in defending against brute force attacks.

14.1.3 Mitigation Strategies

To mitigate brute force attacks, several best practices can be employed:

- **Use Strong Password Policies**: Organizations should enforce strong password creation policies, requiring a minimum length and a mix of character types.

- **Account Lockout Mechanisms**: Implementing automatic lockout mechanisms after a predefined number of failed attempts can hinder brute force attacks.

- **Employ Rate Limiting**: Limiting the number of authentication attempts in a specific timeframe can significantly reduce the likelihood of a successful brute force attack.

- **Utilize Two-Factor Authentication (2FA)**: The addition of a secondary authentication mechanism can provide an additional layer of security that is not vulnerable to brute force attacks on passwords alone.

14.2 Side-Channel Attacks

Unlike brute force attacks, which directly target the encryption algorithm, side-channel attacks exploit the physical implementation of cryptographic systems. These attacks extract sensitive information from the environment surrounding the encryption process rather than breaking the cryptographic algorithm itself.

14.2.1 Types of Side-Channel Attacks

Side-channel attacks can be categorized into several types, including:

Timing Attacks

Timing attacks leverage variations in the timing taken by a cryptographic operation to infer secret keys. By analyzing the time it takes to execute cryptographic routines, an attacker can deduce valuable information about the key being used.

Power Analysis Attacks

Power analysis attacks monitor the power consumption of a device as it performs cryptographic operations. Variations in power usage can reveal information about the operations being performed, potentially enabling an attacker to recover the cryptographic keys.

Electromagnetic Attacks

These attacks involve monitoring the electromagnetic emissions from a device while it is operating. Just like power analysis, the electromagnetic waves emitted can reveal details about the internal operations, including potentially sensitive information such as cryptographic keys.

14.2.2 Defense Against Side-Channel Attacks

To secure cryptographic systems against side-channel attacks, the following strategies can be employed:

- **Constant-Time Algorithms**: Implement algorithms that execute in a predictable time frame, making it difficult for attackers to glean timing information.

- **Power-Noise Countermeasures**: Include noise generators and power regulators that can mask the actual power consumption patterns during cryptographic operations.

- **Shielding Techniques**: Utilize electromagnetic shielding to reduce the risk of leakage via electromagnetic emissions.

14.3 Fault-Based Attacks

Fault-based attacks, sometimes referred to as fault injection attacks, exploit errors or faults in the cryptographic process to gain access to sensitive data. These errors can be introduced intentionally through various means, such as voltage spikes, electromagnetic interference, or even benign errors in software execution.

14.3.1 Mechanism of Fault-Based Attacks

An attacker might disrupt the cryptographic computation at a crucial moment, causing the system to produce incorrect results. If the faulty execution reveals secrets in the returned output, the attacker can analyze the discrepancies to infer the secret key.

For example, in the case of public key cryptosystems, a fault injected during the decryption process may result in an error that leaks key information. Similarly, attacking symmetric key algorithms during crucial calculation stages can yield freestanding bits of the key.

14.3.2 Examples of Fault-Based Attacks

- **Differential Fault Analysis (DFA)**: Involves inducing faults during the encryption process and analyzing the difference between the correct and faulty outputs to recover the secret key.

- **Simple Fault Attacks (SFA)**: Here, a single fault is induced, allowing the attacker to derive crucial insights from the erroneous output.

14.3.3 Prevention Strategies

To counter fault-based attacks, various

measures can be taken:

- **Error Detection Codes**: Implementing error detection mechanisms can help identify when a fault has occurred, thus preventing further exposure of sensitive data.

- **Redundancy and Diversity**: Performing cryptographic operations redundantly across multiple paths or using different algorithms can mitigate the risk that a single fault can lead to sensitive information being compromised.

- **Robust Hardware**: Using specially designed hardware that is resistant to fault injection attacks can significantly enhance the security of cryptographic systems.

While encryption remains one of the most powerful tools in cybersecurity, understanding its vulnerabilities is critical to ensuring data protection. Brute force attacks utilize sheer computational power to crack passwords and keys, while side-channel attacks exploit the physical characteristics of cryptographic implementations. Fault-based attacks introduce erroneous conditions that, if exploited correctly, can lead to significant data breaches.

By incorporating robust defenses against these types of attacks, organizations can bolster their cryptographic systems, ultimately mitigating the risks associated with encrypted data. Awareness and education about these vulnerabilities and attack vectors are essential steps in the fight against cyber threats in an increasingly digital world. As technology continues to evolve, so too must our strategies for protecting sensitive information, reinforcing the need for adaptive and resilient encryption solutions.

Chapter 15: Security Audit and Assessment

In our digital age, the significance of security audits and assessments cannot be overstated. Security audits evaluate an organization's information system security and compliance with relevant standards, while security assessments provide an in-depth analysis of vulnerabilities, threats, and the overall effectiveness of security measures. This chapter will delve into security auditing techniques and explore cryptographic standards such as FIPS (Federal Information Processing Standards) and NIST (National Institute of Standards and Technology) that play a crucial role in the protection and integrity of information systems.

15.1 Security Audit Techniques

Security audits can take many forms, and they often encompass various techniques and methodologies tailored to the specific needs of the organization. The goal is to systematically evaluate the effectiveness of security policies, controls, and measures in place. Some common audit techniques include:

15.1.1 Internal Auditing

Internal auditing is conducted by employees within the organization. This approach ensures a deeper understanding of the company's systems, processes, and culture. Internal auditors review existing security policies and practices to identify gaps and recommend improvements.

Benefits:

- Cost-effective and convenient.

- In-depth knowledge of internal processes.

- Greater alignment with organizational goals.

15.1.2 External Auditing

External audits are performed by third-party organizations or independent consultants. This approach provides an impartial assessment of the organization's security measures and compliance levels, as external auditors are not influenced by internal biases or pressures.

Benefits:

- Objective evaluation of security posture.

- Access to auditors' expertise in varied industries.

- Increased credibility with stakeholders.

15.1.3 Compliance Audits

Compliance audits involve the assessment of an organization's adherence to specific regulations, legal frameworks, or industry standards. These audits often focus on particular compliance requirements, such as PCI-DSS (Payment Card Industry Data Security Standard) for organizations that handle sensitive payment information.

Benefits:

- Ensures meeting industry regulations.

- Mitigates risks associated with non-compliance.

- Helps maintain customer trust and confidence.

15.1.4 Risk Assessments

Risk assessments form a critical component of any security audit. They identify potential threats, vulnerabilities, and the associated risks to the organization. This process allows auditors to prioritize security measures based on the likelihood and impact of potential incidents.

Benefits:

- It's proactive rather than reactive.

- Identifies gaps in the current security framework.

- Aids in determining safe resource allocation for security enhancements.

15.1.5 Penetration Testing

Penetration testing, or "pen testing," is an active technique used during security audits where ethical hackers simulate real-world attacks on the organization's systems. This method identifies weaknesses in security controls by exploring how a threat actor might exploit vulnerabilities.

Benefits:

- Real-world simulation provides actionable insights.

- Highlights vulnerabilities before malicious hackers can exploit them.

- Tests incident detection and response mechanisms.

15.1.6 Continuous Monitoring

With the rapid evolution of cyber threats, continuous monitoring has become essential. This technique involves continually scanning and assessing security controls to detect unauthorized activity promptly. Continuous monitoring seeks to provide a real-time analysis of system integrity.

Benefits:

- Immediate detection of potential breaches or weaknesses.

- Ongoing risk assessment.

- Enhances overall resilience against threats.

15.1.7 Security Reviews

Security reviews involve comprehensive evaluations of policies, standards, and previous audit reports to determine the effectiveness and applicability of existing security measures.

Benefits:

- Ensures updated strategies in line with the latest industry standards.

- Facilitates cultural adherence to security protocols.

- Comprehensive understanding of risk management.

15.2 Assessing Security Controls and Measures

Once the audit techniques are applied, organizations must assess the effectiveness of their security controls. Measures for assessment may include:

15.2.1 Documentation Review

Reviewing documentation is essential for understanding policies, procedures, and controls. Auditors examine records for completeness, accuracy, and effectiveness in mitigating risks.

15.2.2 Evidence Collection

Auditors gather relevant evidence to support findings, including access logs, incident reports, network configurations, and policy references.

15.2.3 Interviews and Surveys

Interviews and surveys can provide qualitative assessments of security measures. Engaging staff, stakeholders, and third-party vendors yields valuable insights into practical security measures and areas for improvement.

15.2.4 Benchmarking

Using industry benchmarks allows organizations to compare their security posture against similar entities, helping identify weaknesses and areas of strength.

15.3 Cryptographic Standards

Cryptography forms a backbone of digital security, providing confidentiality, integrity, authentication, and non-repudiation. In this section, we will examine two significant cryptographic standards: FIPS and NIST.

15.3.1 Federal Information Processing Standards (FIPS)

FIPS are U.S. government standards that apply to all federal agencies when it comes to computer security and cryptography. These standards ensure that systems used to handle sensitive information meet specific security requirements:

FIPS Overview:

- Developed by NIST to establish uniform standards.

- Ensures the security, integrity, and interoperability of federal systems.

- Critical for the protection of government and sensitive information.

Key Areas of Focus:

- Cryptographic algorithms and implementations.

- Securing federal information systems.

- The establishment of security requirements for various technologies.

Implementation:

FIPS standards require federal agencies and contractors to use certain cryptographic modules that comply with the specifications set in FIPS 140-2/3 (Security Requirements for Cryptographic Modules). Products that meet these criteria are validated and published in the Cryptographic Module Validation Program (CMVP).

15.3.2 National Institute of Standards and Technology (NIST)

NIST plays a pivotal role in developing

security frameworks and standards, including cryptographic protocols that influence private and public sectors globally.

NIST Overview:

- Part of the U.S. Department of Commerce.

- Aims to promote innovation and industrial competitiveness through standards.

- Publishes a range of documents covering cryptographic techniques and implementations.

Key NIST Publications Related to Cryptography:

- NIST Special Publication 800-53: Security and Privacy Controls for Information Systems and Organizations.

- NIST Special Publication 800-175: Guidelines for the Selection and Use of Advanced Authentication.

- NIST Special Publication 800-90A:

Recommendation for Random Number Generation Using Deterministic Random Bit Generators.

- NIST Special Publication 800-131A: Transitioning the Use of Cryptographic Algorithms and Key Lengths.

Implementation:

Organizations are encouraged to align with NIST guidelines to enhance security posture. This includes adopting the recommended cryptographic algorithms and best practices for key management to strengthen both internal processes and compliance frameworks.

15.4 Conclusion

As organizations increasingly rely on information technology and digital services, the need for robust security audits and assessments becomes imperative. Employing various auditing techniques provides organizations with the necessary insights to bolster their security measures effectively. Furthermore, aligning operations with established cryptographic standards like FIPS and NIST mitigates risks associated with non-compliance, advances the security framework, and fosters a culture of adherence to best practices. In summary, a comprehensive approach to security auditing and assessment, intertwined with cryptographic standards, is the cornerstone for any organization aiming to safeguard its sensitive information and create a secure operational environment.

By ensuring continuous improvement through rigorous audits and assessments aligned with cryptographic and security standards, organizations can stay ahead of evolving cyber threats while maintaining digital trust and assurance among stakeholders.

Chapter 16: Cryptography in Law and Ethics

Cryptography has become an essential element of contemporary society, impacting various domains such as communication, finance, and data security. As technology evolves, the implications of cryptography on law and ethics become increasingly profound and complex. This chapter explores the relationship between cryptography, privacy, data protection, and the regulatory frameworks that govern these areas.

Privacy and Data Protection

In the digital age, the concept of privacy has expanded to encompass not only the right to keep personal information confidential but also to safeguard individuals against unauthorized access and misuse of their data. Cryptography plays a pivotal role in ensuring data privacy. By utilizing encryption techniques, organizations and individuals can protect sensitive information from potential adversaries, including hackers, cybercriminals, and even rogue state actors.

The Role of Cryptography in Privacy

1. **Encryption Basics**: At its core, encryption is the process of transforming readable data, known as plaintext, into an unreadable format called ciphertext, employing algorithms and keys. Only authorized users with the appropriate decryption key can convert the ciphertext back to its original form. This fundamental principle is vital in safeguarding personal information, such as financial records, medical history, and private communications.

2. **End-to-End Encryption**: One of the most effective methods for preserving privacy is end-to-end encryption (E2EE). This system ensures that messages are encrypted on the

sender's device and can only be decrypted by the intended recipient, preventing third parties from eavesdropping. Applications like Signal and WhatsApp utilize E2EE to protect user communications, reinforcing the importance of cryptography in maintaining privacy in personal and professional exchanges.

3. **Data Breach Prevention**: Cryptography is instrumental in preventing data breaches, which have become alarmingly common due to the increasing amount of sensitive data stored online. By encrypting data both at rest and in transit, organizations alleviate the risks associated with unauthorized access. For example, a company that securely encrypts its customer data significantly reduces the potential damage in the event of a cyberattack, as the stolen data would be rendered useless without the corresponding decryption keys.

Legal Frameworks Supporting Privacy

As the significance of cryptography in protecting privacy grows, various legal frameworks have emerged to address the challenges posed by data breaches and the unauthorized use of personal information.

1. **General Data Protection Regulation (GDPR)**: Enforced in May 2018, the GDPR is a comprehensive regulation that governs data protection and privacy in the European Union (EU) and the European Economic Area (EEA). The GDPR emphasizes the importance of security measures, including encryption, requiring organizations to implement appropriate technical and organizational measures to protect personal data. Failure to comply can result in substantial fines, underscoring the legal impetus for adopting robust cryptographic practices.

2. **Health Insurance Portability and Accountability Act (HIPAA)**: In the United States, HIPAA provides standards for the protection of sensitive patient information.

Covered entities and their business associates are mandated to implement safeguards, including encryption, to protect electronic protected health information (ePHI). The regulation's emphasis on securing ePHI illustrates the critical intersection of cryptography and privacy in the healthcare sector.

3. **California Consumer Privacy Act (CCPA)**: As one of the most stringent privacy laws in the U.S., the CCPA grants California residents control over their personal information. The CCPA encourages businesses to adopt measures such as encryption to protect consumer data. It also establishes consumer rights, including the right to know which personal data is being collected and the right to request its deletion, highlighting the importance of privacy protection in an increasingly data-driven world.

Laws and Regulations on Cryptography

As concerns over data privacy and cybersecurity intensify, lawmakers are focusing on establishing regulations that govern the use of cryptography. While these laws aim to promote security and privacy, they may also pose challenges, particularly concerning the balance between individual rights and national security.

Key Regulations and Laws

1. **Export and Import Restrictions**: Cryptography is subject to various export controls, as some algorithms can be used for both commercial and military applications. The Wassenaar Arrangement is an international arms control regime that establishes export controls on conventional weapons and dual-use technologies, including cryptography. Countries, including the U.S., have regulations that restrict the export of

strong encryption technologies without proper licensing due to concerns about national security.

2. **The USA PATRIOT Act**: Enacted in response to the September 11 attacks, the USA PATRIOT Act expanded the government's surveillance capabilities. Among its provisions, law enforcement agencies can compel businesses to provide access to encrypted data. This creates tension between the need for robust encryption to protect privacy and the state's demand for access in the name of security.

3. **The Encryption Debate**: The balance between strong encryption, privacy, and national security has been a contentious issue for decades. Government agencies, including the FBI and NSA, have argued for "backdoors" in encryption systems, which would allow law enforcement to gain access to encrypted communications under specific conditions. Critics contend that introducing

backdoors compromises the security of users, potentially exposing their data to malicious actors and undermining public trust in digital technologies.

Ethical Considerations

The legal frameworks and regulations around cryptography raise several ethical questions regarding its use, access, and security.

1. **The Right to Privacy**: The ethical implications of surveillance and data collection practices often challenge the fundamental right to privacy. Individuals have a right to expect that their personal information is safeguarded against unauthorized access. Ethical considerations urge governments and organizations to prioritize user privacy and implement transparent practices regarding data handling.

2. **Informed Consent**: As organizations

collect and store vast amounts of personal information, obtaining informed consent from individuals becomes crucial. Users must be aware of how their data is being used, the extent of data collection, and the measures in place to protect their information. Ethical practices require organizations to proactively communicate their data policies and provide users with clear options regarding consent.

3. **Responsibility in Encryption Development**: With the rapid innovation in encryption technologies, developers and organizations have an ethical obligation to consider the societal impacts of their creations. This includes anticipating potential misuse of encryption technologies by malicious actors and finding ways to minimize risks while still promoting user privacy and data protection.

4. **Digital Divide**: Access to encryption technologies may not be equitable across socio-economic strata, leading to a digital

divide. Wealthier individuals and organizations may afford advanced encryption solutions, while marginalized communities may lack access to effective protective measures. Ethical considerations must address the need for equitable access to cryptographic tools, ensuring that all individuals, regardless of their socio-economic status, can protect their privacy and personal information.

5. **Whistleblower Protections**: In scenarios where whistleblowers disclose wrongdoing or illegal activities, ethical dilemmas arise surrounding the use of cryptography. Whistleblowers often require anonymity and secure communication channels to expose misconduct without endangering themselves. Ethical considerations include ensuring that cryptographic tools are available for such individuals, as their actions typically serve the greater good and promote accountability.

Cryptography plays an undeniable role in shaping the landscape of privacy, data protection, and cybersecurity. As legal frameworks evolve alongside technological advancements, the interplay between cryptography and law becomes increasingly complex. Striking a balance between privacy rights and national security interests remains a significant challenge; ethical considerations must be at the forefront of discussions surrounding cryptography as we navigate this intricate landscape.

Both individuals and organizations must remain vigilant and advocate for responsible cryptographic practices that uphold privacy, protect data, and respect individual rights. Furthermore, continuous dialogue among lawmakers, industry leaders, and ethical thinkers will be vital in crafting laws and policies that align with societal values in the face of emerging technologies and challenges.

As we advance into a future shaped by digital interactions and data-driven systems, the ethical implications of cryptography will remain central to discussions about privacy, security, and human rights. The ongoing evolution of laws and regulations will undoubtedly impact the way cryptography is used, perceived, and developed, highlighting the need for a nuanced understanding of its role in the broader legal and ethical context.

Chapter 17: The Future of Cryptography

As we delve deeper into the 21st century, the landscape of cryptography is evolving at an unprecedented pace. The technological advancements of recent years, combined with the growing complexities of global digital interactions, have underscored the necessity for robust cryptographic systems. This chapter explores the future of cryptography by examining emerging trends, potential challenges, and the implications of new technologies such as quantum computing and artificial intelligence on cryptographic practices.

1. The Evolution of Cryptography

To understand the future of cryptography, it is essential to appreciate its origins. Historically, cryptography has evolved from simplistic methods of encoding messages to complex algorithms that protect modern communications. The early days of cryptography, characterized by techniques such as the Caesar cipher or the Vigenère cipher, laid the groundwork for more sophisticated systems developed during the World War II era, such as the Enigma machine.

In contemporary times, public-key cryptography, introduced by Whitfield Diffie and Martin Hellman in 1976, revolutionized secure communication. The introduction of RSA (Rivest-Shamir-Adleman) in 1978 provided a practical method for secure data transmission, allowing for digital signatures and secure key exchange. These developments marked a significant leap in cryptography, paving the way for the wide array of cryptographic protocols in use today, such as AES (Advanced Encryption Standard) and TLS (Transport Layer Security).

2. The Role of Quantum Computing

One of the most significant threats to current cryptographic systems is the rise of quantum computing. Quantum computers operate on principles of quantum mechanics, allowing them to perform complex calculations at speeds unattainable by classical computers. This capability poses a particular risk to widely used encryption methods, as quantum algorithms, such as Shor's algorithm, can effectively factor large integers and solve discrete logarithm problems, rendering RSA and similar public-key cryptography vulnerable.

The implications of quantum computing for cryptography have spurred the development of quantum-resistant algorithms. NIST (National Institute of Standards and Technology) has initiated a post-quantum cryptography project to standardize new cryptographic algorithms that are secure against quantum attacks. Researchers are investigating lattice-based, hash-based, and code-based cryptographic systems, among others, to provide a robust defense against the impending quantum threat.

As we approach the era of practical quantum computing, organizations and governments worldwide are investing heavily in research and development to transition to quantum-resistant cryptographic systems. This transition is expected to take time and will likely lead to a dual systems approach, where both classical and quantum-resistant algorithms co-exist during the transition period.

3. The Rise of Artificial Intelligence

Artificial intelligence (AI) is another transformative force in the realm of cryptography. Machine learning algorithms can analyze vast datasets, identify patterns, and predict outcomes, which can be both a boon and a bane for cryptographic security. On one hand, AI can help strengthen cryptographic systems by automating vulnerability assessments, detecting anomalies in network traffic, and enhancing encryption methods through advanced algorithms. On the other hand, adversaries can employ AI for offensive strategies, such as automated brute-force attacks or the development of sophisticated phishing schemes designed to undermine traditional security measures.

The integration of AI into cryptographic practices also raises ethical concerns. As AI systems become more pervasive, the challenge of ensuring the security and privacy of data stored and processed by these systems becomes paramount. Developing cryptographic methods that can safeguard sensitive information while still allowing AI systems to function effectively will be a critical area of focus in the coming years.

4. Ubiquitous Encryption

As society becomes increasingly reliant on

digital communication and data storage, the concept of ubiquitous encryption will gain prominence. The demand for secure communication channels will lead to the adoption of encryption as a default mechanism in various applications, from messaging apps to cloud storage solutions. This widespread implementation of encryption will provide a stronger defense against data breaches and cyber threats.

However, ubiquitous encryption also comes with challenges. Law enforcement agencies and governments are expressing concerns about the "going dark" phenomenon, where encrypted communications hinder their ability to investigate and prevent criminal activities. This has sparked debates about the balance between privacy rights and public safety, leading to discussions about the need for regulatory frameworks that address the complexities of encryption without compromising its integrity.

In response to these challenges, some tech companies are exploring the concept of "responsible encryption," which allows for secure communication while enabling backdoor access for law enforcement in certain situations. Balancing the demands for security, privacy, and law enforcement access will continue to be a contentious issue as encryption becomes more deeply woven into the fabric of society.

5. The Internet of Things (IoT) and Cryptography

The proliferation of IoT devices presents unique challenges for cryptography. As everyday objects become interconnected through the internet, the volume of data transmitted between devices increases exponentially. This interconnectedness necessitates robust encryption protocols to protect sensitive data and ensure the integrity of communications.

However, many IoT devices are resource-constrained, with limited processing power and memory. This poses a challenge for traditional cryptographic algorithms, which can be computationally intensive. Researchers are working on developing lightweight cryptographic algorithms designed specifically for IoT applications, enabling secure communication without overburdening the devices.

Furthermore, the deployment of blockchain technology within IoT ecosystems has opened new avenues for secure data exchange. Blockchain's decentralized nature and cryptographic components provide a promising framework for ensuring the authenticity and integrity of data exchanged among IoT devices. As the IoT landscape grows, integrating cryptographic solutions with blockchain technology can bolster security and trust in these systems.

6. The Role of Regulation and Standards

As cryptography continues to evolve, the role of regulation and established standards becomes increasingly significant. The rapidly changing technological landscape necessitates adaptive regulatory frameworks that can address emerging challenges while promoting innovation. Governments and international organizations face the task of creating policies that protect citizens' digital rights, promote cybersecurity, and foster technological advancement.

Standardization plays a crucial role in ensuring interoperability among different cryptographic systems. Organizations like NIST are at the forefront of developing cryptographic standards that facilitate trust and security across various platforms. In a globalized digital economy, establishing internationally recognized standards can help mitigate risks posed by cyber threats and promote collaboration among nations in addressing common challenges.

7. Ethical Considerations in Cryptography

The ethical implications of cryptography cannot be overlooked as we move forward. The ability to protect data and communications is a double-edged sword; while it empowers individuals and organizations to safeguard their privacy, it can also enable malicious actors to conduct illicit activities without detection. Striking a balance between granting individuals their right to privacy and ensuring public safety will require ongoing dialogue among stakeholders, including technologists, policymakers, and ethicists.

Additionally, the potential misuse of cryptographic technologies, such as end-to-end encryption, raises questions about accountability and responsibility. As technology continues to advance, the development of ethical guidelines and frameworks will be essential in guiding the responsible use of cryptography.

8. Conclusion: Envisioning the Future

The future of cryptography is undoubtedly intertwined with advancements in technology, evolving societal norms, and global challenges. As we confront the realities of quantum computing and the increasing prevalence of AI, the cryptographic community must remain agile and innovative, developing new algorithms and methodologies that can withstand emerging threats.

The adoption of ubiquitous encryption will enhance the security of digital communications, yet it will also necessitate discussions on regulatory frameworks that balance privacy and law enforcement needs. The integration of cryptography within IoT ecosystems, fueled by developments in blockchain technology, holds promise for securing the next generation of interconnected devices.

As we gaze into the future, the path forward is clear: cryptography will continue to play a pivotal role in safeguarding digital interactions, fostering trust, and protecting individuals' rights. The collaborative efforts of technologists, policymakers, and ethicists will be crucial in shaping a secure and ethical digital future. The story of cryptography is far from over; it is merely entering a new chapter, one filled with both challenges and opportunities.

Chapter 18: Cryptographic Terms

Cryptography is a vast field that encompasses a wide range of concepts, techniques, and terminologies. In this chapter, we aim to define and explain key terms that are fundamental to understanding cryptographic methodologies, their applications, and the underlying principles that govern data security and privacy.

1. Cryptography

At its core, cryptography is the science and art of transforming information to keep it secure from adversaries. It involves creating written or generated codes that allow information to be kept secret. The primary goals of cryptography are to ensure data confidentiality, integrity, and authenticity.

2. Plaintext

Plaintext refers to any data or message that is in its original, readable format prior to encryption. It can include anything from a simple text document to complex data files. The security of cryptographic systems heavily relies on safeguarding plaintext from unauthorized access.

3. Ciphertext

Ciphertext is what results from the encryption of plaintext. It is the encoded output that appears as a random sequence of symbols or bits, making it unreadable to anyone who does not possess the decryption key. When plaintext is transformed into ciphertext, the original message is concealed, thus providing confidentiality.

4. Key

A cryptographic key is a piece of information that determines the output of a cryptographic algorithm. It is an essential part of both the encryption and decryption processes. The strength and length of the key often directly influence the security of the cryptographic system. Keys can be symmetric (the same for both encryption and decryption) or asymmetric (different for each process).

5. Encryption

Encryption is the process of converting plaintext into ciphertext using a cryptographic algorithm and a key. This transformation is designed to prevent unauthorized access to the data. There are various encryption algorithms, including symmetric and asymmetric encryption methods, each with its own characteristics and use cases.

6. Decryption

Decryption is the reverse process of encryption; it involves converting ciphertext back into plaintext using a key. Only those who have the appropriate key can perform decryption, thereby ensuring that sensitive information remains secure.

7. Symmetric Encryption

Symmetric encryption is a type of encryption where the same key is used for both encryption and decryption. This method is efficient and is commonly used for encrypting large amounts of data. However, the key must be kept secret between the communicating parties to ensure security.

8. Asymmetric Encryption

Asymmetric encryption, also known as public-key cryptography, uses a pair of keys: a public key for encryption and a private key for decryption. This model allows secure communication without the need to share secret keys in advance, making it particularly useful for establishing secure channels over insecure networks.

9. Hash Function

A hash function is a one-way cryptographic function that converts an input (or 'message') into a fixed-size string of characters, which looks random. Hash functions are commonly used in various applications, including data integrity verification, password storage, and digital signatures. They are designed to be fast and irreversible, meaning it should be computationally infeasible to reverse the process.

10. Digital Signature

A digital signature is a cryptographic technique that provides the authenticity and integrity of a message. It is composed of a hash of the message that is encrypted using the sender's private key. The recipient can then verify the signature using the sender's public key, ensuring that the message has not been altered and confirming the identity of the sender.

11. Certificate Authority (CA)

A Certificate Authority is a trusted entity that issues digital certificates, which are used to verify the identity of organizations and individuals. These certificates ensure that public keys belong to the entities they assert to belong to, thereby establishing trust in electronic communications.

12. Key Management

Key management refers to the processes and

mechanisms that manage cryptographic keys, including their generation, storage, distribution, and disposal. Effective key management is crucial for maintaining the security of cryptographic systems and ensuring that keys are not compromised.

13. Cryptanalysis

Cryptanalysis is the study of methods for breaking cryptographic codes and systems to recover the plaintext from ciphertext without knowing the key. Cryptanalysts use a variety of techniques to discover vulnerabilities in cryptographic algorithms, which is vital for improving security measures.

14. Block Cipher

A block cipher is a symmetric key cipher that encrypts data in fixed-size blocks (e.g., 128 bits). The same key is used to encrypt each block, and the process can involve various modes of operation to handle data that is longer than a single block.

15. Stream Cipher

A stream cipher is another form of symmetric encryption that encrypts plaintext one bit or byte at a time. Stream ciphers can be faster than block ciphers and are typically used in applications where data is being streamed or transmitted continuously.

16. Initialization Vector (IV)

An initialization vector is a fixed-size input to a cryptographic algorithm that is used to ensure that the same plaintext encrypts to different ciphertexts each time it is encrypted. It adds an element of randomness to the encryption process, improving security.

17. Salting

Salting is a technique used in hashing to add randomness to the input. When storing passwords, for example, a unique salt is generated and added to each password before hashing, ensuring that even if two users have the same password, their hashed values will be different.

18. Public Key Infrastructure (PKI)

Public Key Infrastructure is a framework that enables secure, scalable, and manageable digital communication through the use of public key cryptography. PKI includes policies, hardware, software, and people involved in managing digital certificates and keys.

19. Perfect Secrecy

Perfect secrecy is a theoretical concept in cryptography wherein a ciphertext produced from a plaintext reveals no information about the plaintext itself, regardless of how much computational power an adversary has. The only known system that achieves perfect secrecy is the one-time pad, where the key is as long as the message.

20. Entropy

In the context of cryptography, entropy refers to the measure of randomness or unpredictability in a system. High entropy is crucial for generating secure cryptographic keys, as predictable keys can be easier for adversaries to guess or compute.

21. Man-in-the-Middle Attack (MitM)

A Man-in-the-Middle attack occurs when an attacker intercepts and potentially alters communication between two parties without their knowledge. Effective cryptographic protocols employ measures such as digital signatures and authentication to mitigate the risk of MitM attacks.

22. Transport Layer Security (TLS)

Transport Layer Security is a protocol that ensures privacy and data integrity between two communicating applications. It is widely used to secure communications over the Internet, such as HTTPS for secure web browsing.

23. Secure Sockets Layer (SSL)

SSL is the predecessor to TLS and served a similar purpose in securing internet communications. With vulnerabilities discovered over time, SSL is considered obsolete, and its usage has been largely replaced by TLS.

24. Zero-Knowledge Proof

A zero-knowledge proof is a cryptographic method by which one party can prove to another party that a statement is true without revealing any specific information about the statement itself. This concept is vital in privacy-preserving protocols and authentication systems.

25. Multi-Factor Authentication (MFA)

Multi-Factor Authentication is an authentication method that requires users to verify their identity through multiple means. It typically combines something they know (like a password), something they have (like a smartphone or token), and sometimes something they are (biometric data).

26. Security Tokens

Security tokens are physical or digital devices that authenticate an individual's identity electronically. They can be used in conjunction with passwords to provide a second layer of security.

27. Key Escrow

Key escrow is a security mechanism where a third party holds a copy of the cryptographic keys, enabling access under specific circumstances. While it provides a recovery option, it raises concerns regarding privacy and unauthorized access.

28. Non-repudiation

Non-repudiation is a concept that ensures that a party cannot deny the authenticity of their signature on a document or a message, providing legal assurance that is crucial in electronic transactions.

29. Quantum Cryptography

Quantum cryptography employs the principles of quantum mechanics to secure communication. It offers unprecedented security levels due to the nature of quantum states, making it theoretically secure against any computational attack.

30. Cipher Modes

Cipher modes refer to the specific methods used to encrypt data with block ciphers. Some common modes include:

- **ECB (Electronic Codebook)**: Simplest mode, where each block is encrypted independently.

- **CBC (Cipher Block Chaining)**: Each block is XORed with the previous ciphertext before being encrypted, providing better security than ECB.

- **CTR (Counter Mode)**: Treats the block cipher as a stream cipher, encrypting consecutive counter values.

- **GCM (Galois/Counter Mode)**: Provides both confidentiality and integrity and is widely used in secure communications.

In concluding this chapter, it is essential to recognize that cryptographic terms represent the building blocks of the field. Understanding these terms and concepts is crucial for anyone engaged in information security, software engineering, or related disciplines. The terminology serves not merely as jargon but as a shared language that facilitates clear communication about securing data against unauthorized access and ensuring trust in digital communications. As technologies evolve and cyber threats grow more sophisticated, a solid grasp of cryptographic fundamentals will remain indispensable in safeguarding sensitive information in our increasingly interconnected world.

In future chapters, we will delve deeper into practical applications, case studies, and the evolving landscape of cryptography, exploring how these fundamental terms apply in real-world scenarios and emerging technologies.

Index

www.ingramcontent.com/pod-product-compliance
Lightning Source LLC
LaVergne TN
LVHW051439050326
832903LV00030BD/3169